THE MISTER ROGERS®
PARENTING RESOURCE BOOK

MISTER ROGERS®
PARENTING
RESOURCE BOOK

by *Fred Rogers*

With an introduction by Joanne Rogers

COURAGE BOOKS

AN IMPRINT OF RUNNING PRESS
PHILADELPHIA • LONDON

9   8   7   6   5   4   3   2   1
Digit on the right indicates the number of this printing

Library of Congress Control Number: 2005922309

ISBN 0-7624-2358-7

Cover design by Alicia Freile
Illustrations by Maureen Rupprecht
Interior design by Alicia Freile
Edited by Melissa Wagner
Typography: Century Schoolbook, Frutiger, and VAG Rounded

This book may be ordered by mail from the publisher.
But try your bookstore first!

Published by Courage Books, an imprint of
Running Press Book Publishers
125 South Twenty-second Street
Philadelphia, Pennsylvania 19103-4399

Visit us on the web!
www.runningpress.com
www.fci.org

This book was previously published as two seperate volumes:
The Mister Rogers Parenting Book and *Mister Rogers' Playtime.*

Foreword

Fred was one of those people who loved learning. As long as I've known him, he spent his early mornings and most of his evenings reading and studying. You might find it ironic that he rarely watched TV even though he's best known for his work on television. He would much rather read so that he could deepen his understanding of children and families. And he loved passing along what he learned.

While most people know him as "Mister Rogers," Fred didn't consider himself an actor or an entertainer. His work just happened to be on television. He always thought of himself as a communicator. One of the things that touched him most was to hear from parents who thought of him as a "friend of the family."

It was through Fred's studies with Dr. Margaret McFarland at the Child Development Graduate School of the University of Pittsburgh, that he learned what it meant to communicate with and about children. I remember Margaret saying that one of Fred's greatest strengths was his extraordinary ability to remember what it was like to be a child. She encouraged him to work directly with young children, and that's when he came to understand what it means to talk *with* children—and really listen. Under her guidance, he started to

translate the complexities of child development theory into everyday language.

Fred was also very much aware that we all bring a wide variety of backgrounds, experiences, and feelings to our parenting—and he respected those differences. That's why his approach was never like a "recipe book." He wanted, instead, to share insights about children and parents that he gained from his studies and lifelong learning in child development and family dynamics. He trusted that caring families would use that insight to find their *own* ways to work through their everyday situations and challenges. He also trusted that they would recognize when they needed some advice or help. I remember Fred often saying that asking for help isn't a sign of weakness—it's a sign of real strength.

When he founded his nonprofit production company, Fred named it "Family Communications, Inc" (FCI). That's what he hoped would come out of anything that FCI produced—healthy family communication. He always thought of the "Neighborhood" television programs and songs and books as a beginning...a springboard that would encourage children and parents to talk about their feelings and concerns.

You'll find that same approach in the two companion books that make up this volume—*The Mister Rogers Parenting Book* and *Mister*

Rogers' Playtime Book. Fred filled this resource full of insights about children and parenting, and loaded it with helpful hints and activity ideas—and lots of opportunities for family communication.

In the pages of this book you'll also find stories from parents. Fred loved stories. He learned a lot from what people shared with him of their experiences as parents. Some of the stories came through the fan mail over the years. Some came from people he met along the way—even from people who came up to us when we were in restaurants or airports! Anyone who ever met him still talks about what a remarkable listener he was. He had a way of making people feel comfortable sharing their life experiences, their joys and their concerns with him. In turn they trusted him with the stories of their "inner dramas." I think that's one of the things that makes this book so rich—you'll hear from people who shared with him the ups and downs of their family life.

Much of Fred's life was spent at Family Communications, and I'm grateful now to be connected with his work there. Fred deeply appreciated his dedicated staff. As Chairperson of the board of FCI, I'm proud to be working with them on new ways to continue Fred's legacy.

We're especially pleased that Running Press wanted to connect with us again to offer these two volumes together as a new resource for parents. Thanks to all FCI staff who are involved in every project they produce, in one way or another, and especially to, two FCI staff members, Hedda Bluestone Sharapan and Cathy Cohen Droz, who worked closely with Fred on the original books. A special thanks goes to Dr. Roberta Schomburg, who, as part of her work as consultant to FCI over the years, provided a wealth of activities that were especially valuable for this project. We're also grateful to Dr. Nancy Curry and Dr. Jerlean Daniel, who have contributed much to FCI as consultants and as board members. The Rogers family and the FCI "family" hope this book can be the start of some healthy and helpful communication in your family.

—Joanne Rogers

Table of Contents

Mister Rogers Playtime

Other books by Fred Rogers:

The Giving Box

You Are Special (Miniature Edition™)

The Mister Rogers Parenting Book

Mister Rogers' Playtime

THE MISTER ROGERS® PARENTING BOOK

Helping to Understand Your Young Child

by Fred Rogers

Acknowledgments

We learn about parenting from our own parents, so this book could easily be dedicated to my parents. I'm deeply grateful for them—and my grandparents—who really valued childhood. Through their loving guidance, they've given me a deep appreciation for those early years of life and for the joys and challenges of parenting.

As a father, I am also grateful for how much my wife and I have grown from being parents to our sons and grandparents to our grandsons. Of course, there were times in our parenting that we wish we'd done something differently, but we've tried not to feel too guilty about that. One thing's sure is that we always cared and we always tried our best.

Our "Neighborhood" psychological consultant, Dr. Margaret McFarland, guided our work with wisdom and generosity. It was she who first helped me understand the critical importance of family relationships as well as empathy for childhood. Margaret's ability to understand the complex development of human personality as well as making that understanding comprehensible to her students were rare and precious gifts to all of us.

Dr. Nancy Curry, a close friend and colleague, is forever generous in sharing her wealth of experience from years of working directly with young children, teaching and mentoring university students, and consulting with families. We are grateful to her for reading this manuscript and offering her most thoughtful comments.

Here at Family Communications, my great thanks go to Hedda Bluestone Sharapan whose personal dedication to every phase of this work allowed this book to come to life, and to Cathy Cohen Droz for her constant attention as the words and pictures came together.

We're also grateful to Barry Head for giving us a rich legacy of anecdotes and for helping us communicate with parents in earlier years. As we worked on this manuscript, it was especially helpful to be able to turn to our long-time consultant Dr. Roberta Schomburg and to a young mother on our staff, Britanny Loggi-Smith. And special thanks to all of our Family Communications staff who help us every day in many ways, both seen and unseen.

We're grateful to our friends at Running Press. From the very beginning, Buz Teacher, who's a father himself, gave us encouragement and support. Our editor, Melissa Wagner, brought warmth and enthusiasm along with her thoughtful editorial suggestions. Special thanks to our designer, Alicia Freile, for her patience and her dedication in making these pages look so good. Maureen Rupprecht's illustrations always add extra warmth and sensitivity to our words.

Through the years many parents have shared their experiences and ideas with us through letters, telephone conversations, e-mail, and in person. Their stories have helped me to realize over and over that those of us dedicated to "parenting" are never ever alone.

Introduction

Children grow in all sorts of remarkable ways between the ages of three and six. What an exciting and important time in all areas of their lives! Day by day, they're able to do more and more things. They have better use of their hands and feet so they naturally are better able to manipulate things like crayons and blocks, as well as run, skip, and ride toys with pedals. All that growing feels so good.

It's an exciting and important time for parents, too, because as children are better able to express their thoughts and feelings, we can share in their sense of wonder. Children help to open our eyes with their natural curiosity. Since they don't have much of a sense of cause and effect or what's real and what isn't, they're full of creative interpretations—and misinterpretations! What a special time for parents who are listening to their children's questions and conclusions! Children give us the great gift of a fresh, intriguing look at the world.

Of course these early years are also challenging both for children and for parents. Young children are full of feelings, and those feelings are often hard to express and hard to control. Children aren't born with self-control. They need a lot of help as they try to find appropriate ways to express their feelings.

In their social world, they're learning what it means to be a "friend," but they're still ego-centric. They aren't yet able to see things from someone else's perspective, so sharing and getting along with others can be difficult.

Young children are looking to parents for help in understanding the world, their relationships with others, and their perplexing inner feelings. It's part of normal development for children at times to be demanding, fearful, and, once in a while, aggressive. They often ask very challenging questions. In essence, children are saying to us, "You're the grownups. You know about all those things. You need to help me. I'm just a child."

Echoes from Our Childhood

It can be such a challenge, though, to understand just what kind of help children need from us in dealing with everyday family situations, new experiences, and especially challenging times. Of course you already have one of the most important resources built into your parenting: *you were a child once yourself!*

Because we adults were once children, we have lived through the same early childhood years that our children are going through. We've had children's feelings. We may not remember them consciously; nevertheless, those feelings are somewhere inside of us.

We may have forgotten what it's like not to

be able to reach the light switch, or how it feels to be in the midst of a temper tantrum, but those memories are still there, and they can bubble up within us just from seeing or hearing something that our children say or do.

Since we were children once, the roots for our empathy are already planted within us. We've known what it was like to feel small and powerless, helpless and confused. When we can feel something of what our children might be feeling, it will help us begin to figure out what our children need from us.

Early childhood is the most important part of life. It informs all that we do thereafter. All our lives, we rework the same struggles from our childhood—needing to feel loved, finding a healthy balance between independence and dependence, being able to handle separation from loved ones, dealing with aggression, and working on self-control.

Each time we rework those struggles, we have another chance at coming to a greater mastery over them. When we become parents, just being involved in our children's struggles evokes another reworking in us. *As parents, we have another chance to grow.* And if we can bring our children understanding, comfort, and hopefulness when they need this kind of support, then they are more likely to grow into adults who can find these resources within themselves later on.

Insight into Childhood

Since most of us aren't able to remember many specifics from our earliest years, we're grateful for people in the field of child development who are constantly learning about how children grow, learn, and cope with ordinary and extraordinary happenings at different stages of their lives.

The closer we can come to understanding what our children might be feeling, the more empathic towards them we can become. Instead of taking children's misbehavior personally, for instance, we can begin to understand why it might be happening. Understanding invariably leads to finding caring ways to help.

While empathy allows us to see things from our child's point of view, we still need to keep our own adult perspective as the parent. Even though we might remember how angry we were as children when an adult told us to stop playing and get ready for bed, we need to balance that empathy with our being a limit-setting parent by saying something like, "I know you're having a lot of fun and you don't want to stop playing, but it's still your bedtime." Children really do want their parents to make rules and set limits—even though they might "test" us. They want—and need—their parents to be in charge.

Even power struggles with toddlers tend to be misinterpreted as a statement that "My child is out to get me." But the more we learn that it's natural—and necessary—for toddlers to assert their autonomy, the more we can recognize that our child's defiant "no's" are probably telling us, "I need to be a separate human being!" Then, depending on the situation, we might be better able to think of appropriate choices (or maybe even distractions) to break the power struggle, all the while remaining the "adult in charge."

Family Communication

There are no scripts or recipes for ongoing caring communication with children. Each child is unique. Each parent is unique. What works with one child in a family may not work for another one.

Nevertheless, communicating grows out of "being there" and letting our children know we care about them. Whether a child is talking, playing, dancing, building, singing, or painting, if we care, we can try to listen. Children communicate in many ways through what they do and how they react to what we do.

Of course, all human beings communicate through much more than words. We let people know how important something is to us just by the way we look at it, pay attention to it, and move toward it. Our bodies are as expressive as our words. For instance, sometimes when children are frightened they can feel security simply in the loving touch of our hand on theirs.

For children to feel secure, our communication with them needs to be consistent. It's only natural, though, that there will be times that mothers and fathers might deal with situations differently, and children can generally handle that. But children need to know what to expect from each parent day by day. Children also need to understand that each person, even each parent, is different.

If parents can talk with each other about their attitudes and values and about rules and discipline, they can become more comfortable with each other's ideas. Of course parents won't always be able to agree—and that's something they have to accept—but talking can help keep the disagreements within manageable limits. No mothers and fathers were ever raised in exactly the same ways by their parents, and all of us bring echoes from our own childhoods to the task of raising our children.

Communicating is a process in which we learn more about our children and more about ourselves. It's another way that parenting gives us a new chance to grow.

Family Life Is Full of Feelings

Of course, family communication also includes times when we get angry with our children and times that our children get angry with us. That's a part of being human. In fact, one of the songs in our *Neighborhood* program is about the close connection between love and anger. The song starts with "It's the people you like the most who can make you feel gladdest." The second verse is, "It's the people you like the most who can make you feel maddest." Finding constructive ways to express our anger, whether we're parents or children, is one of life's important jobs.

The anger we feel toward our children often comes from our own needs. When a child embarrasses us in the store, we feel others are looking at us and thinking, "What a bad parent!" Or maybe after we've spent a lot of time and effort to make a particular mealtime dish, our child says, "Yuck!" and refuses to eat it. That can make us feel that it's not only our food that's being rejected, but we ourselves as well. Sometimes when our children are dependent and whining, we might feel our own impulses to be plaintive and demanding, too. We don't like it. We don't want to be reminded of those feelings in us, and so we might even surprise ourselves by reacting really strongly to our children's whining.

When we begin to understand some of the many feelings we bring to our parenting, we can be more forgiving of ourselves. We want to think of ourselves as nurturing people.

With all the stresses of family life, it can be helpful to set aside some "alone time" somewhere in the day—time all by yourself. You're the most important person in your child's life, and if you do what you can to nourish yourself, deeply and simply, you'll have more energy for nourishing your child.

Just a Phase?

Often it's hard to know the difference between something that's "just a phase" in the development of your child and something that needs more professional help. You may find it reassuring to hear from other parents that they're dealing with the same things, or to hear that others have grown past similar struggles so you can feel hopeful that this "phase" may soon pass just as it did for other people's children.

If you have a persisting problem, it could help to talk with a childcare provider or early childhood or kindergarten teacher who knows your child and you. Early childhood specialists can usually sense what's normal behavior and what may need extra intervention.

When we can't understand a problem and feel it's getting beyond our abilities to cope, it's important to reach out for help. Asking for help is a sign of real strength. There are people in almost every community who have chosen the understanding of children as their life's work. You may want to seek them out, get to know them, and let them get to know you and your children. The most meaningful advice can come from professionals who know us and who care about us.

We Grow Little by Little

Parents don't come full bloom at the birth of the first baby. In fact, parenting is about growing. It's about our own growing as much as our children's growing and that kind of growing happens little by little. It's tempting to think "a little" isn't significant and that only "a lot" matters. But most things that are important in life start very small and change very slowly, and they don't come with fanfare and bright lights.

Often being a parent forces us to know ourselves better than we ever might have imagined. We're bound to discover some surprising thoughts and feelings inside ourselves, even talents we never dreamed we had. As time goes on, most of us discover that we have more to give and are actually *able* to give more than we ever imagined.

Of course, there are limits to our giving, and we need to feel comfortable in recognizing that we can't be all things to our children. Just as it takes time for children to understand what real love is, it takes time for parents to understand that *always* being patient, quiet, even-tempered, and respectful isn't necessarily what "good parents" are. So-called "perfect parents" and "perfect children" do not exist. "Human parents" and "human children" do— and to you, we dedicate this book.

Everyday Experiences

Day by day, in the secure "nest" of family life, children learn the most essential thing of all—how to live with other people. Daily life requires some structure and routine so that everyone in the family knows what to expect and can move through the day with some comfort and predictability.

That means, of course, that children can't do only what they want to do. There are rules and limits about such things as when we eat, what we eat, and when we sleep. As much as children may "test" the rules, they need—and want—adults to be in charge.

As children deal with the ups and downs of everyday life with parents, brothers or sisters, and friends, they're learning about compromise, responsibility, love, anger, generosity, compassion, and cooperation. Little by little they develop the ability to wait, to share, to try, to cope with disappointment, to understand, and to express feelings. Day by day, they're seeing how they are like other people and how they are different. If they're fortunate, little by little they're coming to realize that they are unique, and that everyone else in this world is unique, too.

As a parent, day in and day out, you're a nurturer, comforter, problem-solver, protector, limit-setter, and much more. In the safety of the family, you're helping your child learn how to get along with others, how to deal with rules and limits, how to cooperate, compromise, and negotiate—all qualities that are essential for whatever relationships may be in your child's future.

Mealtime

"When my daughters saw pitted black olives on the dinner table, they'd stick them on their finger tips and eat the olives off one at a time. My husband and I weren't quite sure how to handle that. We had a rule about not playing with food, and it's hard to know what to be strict about. But the girls weren't making a mess or wasting food, and that's why we had made that rule; we figured that if we let them have that kind of fun with the olives, maybe they would be more willing to go along with our other mealtime rules."

Mealtime means different things to different families, but one thing is sure—food is important to everyone, right from the start.

Food and Love

As newborns, the hurt of hunger is one of the earliest hurts we ever know, and it makes us cry again and again. But each time, if we are fortunate, someone makes that hurt go away by giving us food. Little by little, even the smells, sights, and sounds of the person who feeds us becomes comforting.

Knowing deep within us that someone is going to feed us when we are hungry is how trust and love begin, right at the earliest "mealtimes."

Why So Picky?

As children get older, mealtime can sometimes seem like a battleground between parents and children. Toddlers say "no" to lots of things in their struggle to be their own self. They're not taunting us—it's their way of saying, "I am a separate person." At one moment they may say "no" to the very thing they had agreed to the day before, just because they want to see what the "no" feels like. Of course, their refusals may also be honest reactions to unfamiliar smells, colors, and textures.

If you talk with other parents, you will probably find that many children are picky eaters. Children may even be fussy about the way the food is set out on a plate and won't eat if the peas touch the mashed potatoes! While their reaction may seem to be only about the food, it's probably much more than that. As preschoolers are finding out more and more about their world, they do their best to understand things by putting them into clearly separate categories. They may be just as rigid about the food that's on their plate as they are about needing to "put all the red ones in the red box."

We know a kindergarten teacher who reminds her students' parents of something that's just as important as the food at mealtime—it's the ordinary, everyday conversation that takes place around the table (with the television off and the telephone answering machine on!).

At the dinner table, children learn the art of making conversation—how to take turns listening and talking and how to put their ideas into words. Even their vocabulary increases as they learn new words and new ideas from others in the family. Letting our children know we care about what they have to say is another way to let them know, "I care about **you**." No wonder teachers find that ordinary, everyday mealtime conversation is one of the best preparations for school!

Parents' Feelings of Rejection

One of the first ways parents measure their own success is by how well their infant does at feeding time. By instinct we seem to sense that making sure our children are healthy is one of our most important "jobs." When we feed our children, we seem to be saying to them, "I care about you," and saying to ourselves, "I'm a good parent!" That's why most parents spend a lot of time thinking about what foods to buy and what meals to make. From early on, we're heavily invested in feeding and eating!

It's only natural that you want your children to like the foods you make for them. After all, it's part of yourself that you're offering. You've given your time and your energy to all the work of buying, preparing, and serving a meal. A toddler turning down food can bring parents a feeling of personal rejection that goes much deeper than the rejection of the peas or carrots.

Mealtime Is Family Time

There are lots of things that families struggle with at dinnertime. Grownups and children may have hectic days, and they're tired from all they've done all day long. At times like that, it's harder to be patient and understanding. Since mealtimes have such deep meanings about relationships and love and giving and receiving, it's worth all the effort it takes to avoid turning mealtimes into bargaining sessions or battlegrounds.

That's not to say that parents should be so permissive that they allow their children to eat badly, irregularly, or not at all. Far from it! Part of responsible and caring parenting is helping children develop healthy eating habits. There's often a good deal of leeway in how we can do that.

Dealing with Picky Eaters

Some parents wonder if they should prepare different meals for their picky eaters. As with most things in parenting, there are no easy answers to that question, but unless a child is ill and can't tolerate certain foods, it doesn't seem to make a lot of sense to spend time and energy making separate meals every night. Of course, each family has to find what works best for its parents and its children. That's how we all learn what it means to compromise.

Most doctors say that children usually eat enough and well enough when they're offered healthy choices. If you're worried about your child's eating habits, you might want to talk with your child's doctor.

It's likely that your child's preferences won't stay the same forever. Most children's food tastes change as they grow. It's possible that you now eat foods you wouldn't touch as a child. Your child will probably find that happening years from now as well.

Helpful Hints

Before the Meal:

■ Mealtime starts before the meal is on the table. Give your child things to do to help get the meal ready, like shopping with you for groceries, choosing vegetables or fruits for the meal, setting the table with napkins and spoons, or putting bread or crackers on a plate. Of course, it can be more time-consuming if you involve your child, but if you do it now and then, you may find that your child is more interested in the meal itself.

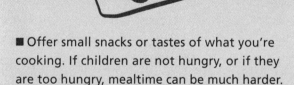

■ Offer small snacks or tastes of what you're cooking. If children are not hungry, or if they are too hungry, mealtime can be much harder.

■ Let your child know about five minutes before dinner will be ready. It's hard to stop playing, so children need time to end what they are doing.

■ When you're setting out the food, remember that children have small stomachs, so give them small servings of food. Children also tend to eat better if there isn't a lot of food in front of them. They like to feel proud when they can finish everything on the plate.

During the Meal:

■ When children have rules, they know what is expected of them. Some families have rules like:

Wash hands before you eat.
No eating until everyone is at the table.
If you don't like a food that's being served, you still have to be kind.
Ask to be excused before you get up from the table.
Hold hands and offer a prayer or "thank you" before a meal.

■ Many families have rules about tasting new foods. You may want to suggest taking just a small bite, saying something like, "You don't have to like it, but at least you tried." Some children like to try new foods. Others don't, and forcing only upsets them.

■ Have some fun meals, like:
Leftover night
Make your own sandwich, taco, or pizza
Breakfast foods for supper

■ Some families have a tradition of eating particular foods on certain days of the week. With so many changes in everyday life, it can help when some things stay just the same.

Choosing Playthings

"It really upset me when my four-year-old started playing about guns. He'd grab a toy, point it, and run around the house saying, "Bang! Bang! You're dead!" But I know that children need to work all kinds of things out for themselves through play. I've told him how I feel about real guns, and I won't buy any toy guns. If he makes them from his plastic toys or his fingers, at least it's coming from him—and not from me."

Children's play depends on what they're thinking about or dealing with at that moment. They might play to try on different roles, figure out what the world is like, or work through some of their feelings and concerns. Or they may want to play just for fun.

That's why the very best kinds of playthings are open-ended: blocks or stuffed animals, toy cars, or play clay and art supplies. Children can make of them whatever they're working on at that moment, and their play is then determined by their own needs. If most of their playthings are "single-action" toys, their play tends to be limited, as if they're following the "formula" of what the manufacturer determined.

Play Themes

While children play with a wide variety of things and use them in uniquely different ways, there are usually just a few themes that children play about over and over again. In the preschool years, children play mainly about "going away and coming back," "power and control," "good guy versus bad guy," "nurturing and being nurtured," and "chase and rescue." All of these themes are naturally related to the things that they are working on in their everyday lives.

When children play about making their toy cars go away and come back, they may be dealing with the feelings they have each time their parents go away for work or for an evening out. In their real lives, children are the ones who are left behind and left wondering when and if their parents will return. When they play, the children are the ones who are in charge of when things go away and when they come back. As they play about such things over and over again with their toys, they come to trust that things—and people—can and will return.

Playing with those same toy cars can also be a help if children are working on self control. If they can manage to keep their toy cars on a track made of blocks or masking tape, they can also start to feel that they're able to keep something else within bounds—their own aggressive urges. If a household is disorganized because of a move to a new home, a child living there might line up all his or her toy cars in a row, needing to create some order, at least with the toys.

Children often use dolls or stuffed animals to try out what it feels like to be mothers and fathers who care for babies, prepare meals, and make rules. Children sometimes play about being mothers and fathers who punish little ones. There may be times when children play about being babies, sucking on toy baby

I watched a four-year-old playing with a toy airplane, making it swoop and dive over and over again. Then he stopped and looked into the plane's empty cockpit. He couldn't find any little toy figures that could fit into the pilot's seat, so he took a small wooden cylinder from a block set and used it as the pilot. Creativity and problem-solving growing out of play with simple things help children deal with life's challenges now and later on.

bottles. Playing like that can be a relief from the pressures of being more grown up.

Playing about Power

One of the most compelling play themes in the preschool years is playing about having power—even super power! Children now realize that grownups have power over most things that happen in family life—when and what to eat, when it's okay to play, what's acceptable behavior, and when it's bedtime. Playing about power lets children be in control, at least for the moment.

A natural way for children to play about being powerful is by pretending to be grownup. With dress-up clothes (neckties, long skirts, hats) and grownup props (briefcases, toy telephones, pens and notebooks, cooking bowls and spoons), they can try out what it feels like to be the adults who seem to have all the power.

Children can also feel powerful when they use their playthings to make things happen, like when they construct tall buildings with blocks and knock them down. Or they can enjoy the power of creating a whole world of imagined or real things on paper or with play clay. Even though they don't have a lot of control over the real people or real things around them, children can put their toy figures in different situations and in that way "control" how *those things* act and react.

Aggressive Toys

Unfortunately, many toys are developed with one simplistic message: the way to have power is to have a weapon. Aggressive toys are highly appealing to children whose fantasies are filled with having unlimited power and control. The person with the gun literally "calls the shots."

Toys such as guns, swords, and water pistols give children the clear message that the way to handle conflict is to wipe out the "bad guys" with force. At a time in their lives when they're working on controlling their own aggressive urges, trying as best as they can to keep their own inner "bad guy" in check, it can be very satisfying if they can make sure the

"bad guy" they feel inside is finished off or locked up in jail in their play.

Naturally, superheroes are very popular at this age. Playing about conquering enemies is important because it helps children feel more in control of their natural aggression. But the pretending can sometimes seem too real and scary. Parents need to stop scary play when they see that their children have become overly fearful.

If things get too frightening, children need to be able to rely on their parents to help them understand that the toy alligator's teeth and the monster's growl are just pretend.

Parents are often dismayed that at a certain age their young children turn almost everything they pick up into a "gun." When children play with pretend guns, it doesn't mean that they are likely to grow up to use real ones. Parents who feel uncomfortable about gun play need to let their children know how they feel about it and about anything that involves people hurting each other.

Electronic Games

At their best and used selectively, electronic toys and video games can help children learn, problem-solve, and develop eye-hand coordination. But those toys and games often have limited and repetitive fantasies built into them. There's something very different about physically holding and manipulating three-dimensional toy farm animals, putting them anywhere and pretending they can eat, gallop, or sleep, than maneuvering two-dimensional pictures with very limited movement and options for placement.

Spending a lot of time making canned devices work means less time spent in the rich kind of play that young children need most—play of their own invention, from their own imagination. It really helps a child for his or her parents to set healthy limits for any kind of "electronic" play.

Parents' Role in Encouraging Play

One way we show that we value our children's play is by offering them toys and times that can be used in all sorts of imaginative, creative ways. Children sense that we care about their play when we give them quiet time to play alone or with friends, with no distractions of television or radio.

With a simple suggestion from a parent, almost any toy can expand to another level with a child's imagination. If your child is playing with action-figures, you might want to offer an empty box for your child to make into a house or a car for those figures. If you're concerned about all the "fighting" that's going on between the toy characters, you might want to suggest that your child make a hospital or a home for the wounded people. That can also turn "chase" play into "rescue" play, something that many people in our society want to encourage in the next generation.

As careful as we parents may be about the playthings we offer and the ideas we suggest, children still ask for toys that we might find inappropriate. It can help to remember that just because a child asks for something doesn't mean that he or she really wants it or needs it. Children are easily seduced by television ads and peer pressure, even in the preschool years. As parents, we can be honest and let our children know how we feel about those playthings. In that way, we're letting them know some of the important values of the family to which they belong.

Children's play is their work, and the more we encourage children to play, the more we will be giving them an important resource for learning and for growing all through their lives.

Helpful Hints

■ Children need open-ended toys like blocks, art supplies, little cars and trucks, stuffed animals, and dolls. They can play with those kinds of toys according to whatever is important to them at that moment.

■ Some of the best toys are inexpensive—and even free! A paper towel tube can be a tunnel for cars, a pretend telescope, or a sword. Even a big empty box can give children hours of imaginative play—as a car, plane, or boat. Before throwing something away, consider whether it can be recycled as a plaything. Thinking about everyday "throwaways" as playthings might even re-evoke your own childhood, and that in itself can be one of your greatest gifts to your child.

■ Younger children are more likely to pretend with playthings that resemble the real thing, like realistic looking toy telephones, toy paper money, and plastic dishes and spoons. Because older children tend to have more fully-developed imaginations, they can turn almost anything into something else—a rope becomes a gas pump, a hand on an ear is a phone, or a touch on the palm is enough to pretend there's money being paid.

■ Many parents find that if they store toys in see-through containers, their children are more likely to go to the boxes to find what they need, and that when they're cleaning up, it's easier to know where their playthings belong.

■ Sometimes having too many toys available can be overstimulating and can actually stifle play. To encourage exciting and interesting play, keep your child's toys on a rotating system, periodically stowing some toys away for a while and bringing them back out in exchange for others.

■ Sometimes other children may play about things like monsters or "bad guys" in ways that are scary for your child because it seems too real. Let your child know it's okay to say, "Stop that. I don't want to play that way."

■ Before going to a store, tell your child ahead of time what you're planning to buy, and let your child know that's all you're going to buy. Then saying "no" may be easier for you to say and for your child to accept.

Everyday Rules and Limits

"I'd announce a punishment, like no TV for three nights, and after a little while my son would 'forget' or test me by trying to watch TV with his brother. Sometimes I myself would forget about it completely. Someone suggested writing a note and posting it on the refrigerator, and that really helped. Even though my son was too young to read, all I had to do was point to the note, and he understood. The note helped me remember, too."

No child is born with self-discipline. Right from the start, children need parents to feed them and to keep them healthy and safe until they can manage on their own. In the same way, they need their parents to provide them with the discipline they need until they learn to discipline themselves.

The Importance of Setting Limits

When children are young, they need a lot of limits. Many are for their health and safety—what can be touched and what cannot, what's good to eat and what isn't, where it's safe to play and where it's not. We set other limits to help children live comfortably among other people—what they can say to whom, what they can do and where.

Even though children may act like they want to be in control, they really need and want adults to be in charge. It can be very frightening for children not to have limits. They can become anxious and test the limits even more when their parents "give in" or aren't sure how firm to be.

Not only do children need limits to be safe from dangers in the outside world, they also need limits to help with the inside world of feelings. It can be scary when they aren't sure they can manage their feelings by themselves. They worry that they could hurt the people they love. Children need to trust that their adults

A mother told me about a time when she scolded her daughter and sent her to her bedroom to cool down and think about what she had done. The girl slipped a note under the door. In childlike scrawl she had written, "I hate you mommy!" A bit later, the daughter settled down and came out of her room. When she saw the note, she turned it over and wrote, "I love you mommy." Then she added another line: "I will never hate you as much as I love you." What an important message for both the mother and daughter—that even though they may have times when they are upset with each other over a rule, the love between them will always be strong.

will give them limits, like "no hitting." They need to be able to rely on us to help them stay in control, to know that all of their feelings are okay, and to help them to find constructive ways of expressing their full range of feelings.

Testing the Rules

Even though children may test the limits, they really do feel safer when the people they love have told them what to do and what not to do. Testing limits is the "work" children do in order to learn how serious we adults are about the rules.

Some children more than others seem to test adults and the rules. Their testing is often a signal that they're struggling with the need to assert their separateness from us. For those children, it may be helpful to give some choices (where it's reasonable), along with clear and consistent rules. When children see that they have power over some things, they may not have to fight so hard over other things. If they can choose which pajamas to wear, which stuffed animal to take to bed, and which books are read to them, it may be easier for them to accept their parents' decision about when the bedtime routines start.

The most powerful motivation for children is the desire to be loved. They learn to behave in ways that give their parents pleasure rather than displeasure. It's their continuing love for us that helps them accept healthy discipline from us and that eventually helps them develop their own inner discipline.

Routines and Rules Help Parents

Most parents realize that the most effective way to deal with rules and limits is to provide consistency in family life. But that's much easier said than done!

It can be an enormous challenge to establish some regularity when each day seems to bring new demands. Out of necessity, many families have had to become somewhat casual about routines. However, when children and parents can't count on some structure in everyday life, it's harder to know when to give in and when to stay firm.

It's even difficult for many parents today to figure out which rules really matter. There used to be much clearer boundaries of what was acceptable and what wasn't. Maybe, too, some of our ambivalence about sticking to the rules comes from our own long-ago fear of losing our parents' love. Maybe we're afraid we'll lose the love of our children when we don't let them have their way. But giving them limits while they need them is a loving gift that can be one of the greatest satisfactions of parenting.

With the heavy demands of everyday life, parents today are often concerned that they don't have much time with their children, and they don't want to spend the time they do have fighting over rules. It may seem easier to give in so that things will quiet down and be more pleasant, but that's a short-term solution. If you can manage to stay firm and keep the long term in mind, you're giving your child another opportunity to know that you're serious about the rules, and to realize that the struggle won't get you to back down.

DINNER RULES
Sit in your seat
Use "Inside" voice
Ask to leave the table

It's Hard to Keep Your Cool

Power struggles can be enormously frustrating for parents. How can it be that adults who can control so many other things can't get a three-year-old to stop throwing food on the floor or get a four-year-old to talk respectfully?! It's easy for our powerlessness to turn to anger, and when we act out of anger instead of our children's needs, we may find ourselves doing and saying things we later regret. At times like that "counting to ten" and a sense of humor can be really helpful.

Of course, it's a rare parent who hasn't lost his or her temper with a child. Young children can learn a lot from us when, after the heat of the moment has passed, we can apologize for something we did that was inappropriate. It's good discipline (for us as well as for our children) to be able to say, "I'm sorry I got so angry; I shouldn't have screamed at you," all along being clear about what was wrong with your child's behavior.

A Teaching-Learning Relationship

As its root word "disciple" suggests, discipline is a teaching-learning kind of relationship which depends more on intimacy and trust than on authority. Disciplining includes comfort, care, and nurture. It includes praise for achievement, and it most certainly includes *examples,* from which young children learn so much. When they see us hang up our clothes, clean up before relaxing, or express our anger through words and in non-destructive ways, our children learn through our living examples.

Most importantly, we parents need to try to find the security within ourselves to accept the fact that we and our children won't always like one another's actions. There will be times when we won't be able to be "friends," and there will be times of anger within the family. We need to remember that it's our continuing love for our children that makes us want to help them become the healthiest adults they can possibly be.

Helpful Hints

Making Rules:

■ Choose a few rules that matter most. Children are more likely to know what's expected of them when we tell them the rules simply and clearly, like "hold hands with a grownup when you're crossing the street," "no hitting," "no name-calling," and "ask before you take something."

■ Try to provide some structure to everyday life. "Bedtime at 8:00" is a lot clearer than bedtime whenever your child seems tired, or "a little after your dad gets home," whenever that may be.

■ Children are more likely to go along with a rule when you give a reason for it, even if they don't like your reason or understand it completely. You could say something like, "No running here. I want you to be safe," or "You cannot hit. No hurting in our family," or "You have to be in your car seat. That's the law."

■ When you talk about a rule, be clear with your child about the consequences for breaking the rule. Some families set up consequences like, "if you hit, you go to your room," or "if you throw a toy, it gets taken away."

■ Let your child know that children don't have to *like* the rules, but they still have to *follow* them. When children know you care about their feelings, they are usually better able to manage within the rules.

■ When possible, offer choices. Children test limits because of their own need for independence. When they're allowed to make some of the decisions, they're more likely to go along with the decisions that their parents make.

■ If you're taking your child into a new situation or one that you feel may be difficult, let your child know what to expect and what you expect of him or her.

■ Be sure to give praise when your child follows the rules. That's a caring way for your child to hear how important the rule is to you. By praising your child, you're strengthening the foundation for self-discipline.

When Children Break Rules:

■ When your child seems ready to break a rule, get down to your child's eye level and talk right to him or her. Ask your child to repeat the rule after you. Then you know your child has heard you. Your child is more likely to hear what you say if you use a firm but kind voice rather than if you yell.

■ If there's a misbehavior, try to make the consequences follow right afterwards. Young children can't hold things in their memory for long, and if you say, "Wait till we get home!" they're less likely to understand the connection between what they did and the consequence.

■ If you're in public and your child doesn't follow a rule that you've made (like staying in the cart at the grocery store) firmly but kindly take your child out of the store, even if you have to leave behind what you intended to buy. Your firm actions let your child know that you're serious about the rule.

■ When your child starts to hit someone or throw something but then hesitates and holds back, it's important to say, "I'm really proud of you. I know you were mad, but you found a way to stop." When children are angry, it takes a lot of self-control to stop from hitting or throwing. Any time we can applaud them during a moment of control, we're strengthening their ability to stop when they're about to do something they know is wrong.

■ Make a clear distinction between the behavior and the child. It's so easy to say, "You're a bad boy," but that's not what we want the child to understand. It's the *behavior* that's bad, not the child! Children need to learn to feel good about who they are, and self-discipline (checking the bad things they may feel like doing) helps greatly in the development of that good feeling.

■ If you don't discipline your child for breaking a rule, your child may think that you don't care about the rule, and may just keep breaking the rule to see what you will do. If there are times when you need to give in, let your child know you're changing the rule, but for just that one time.

Television and Children

"When I feel my daughter has seen enough television or videos, I tell her that I am going to make one of her favorite snacks and would like her help. I make some noise getting out bowls, opening and closing cupboards—and pretty soon she turns off the television and joins me in the kitchen. I want her to know that it is more fun making something with other people than watching television alone."

Television can be very confusing to young children. Preschoolers are still trying to figure out how the world works—what is real, what is pretend. Because of its special effects, animation, and sophisticated editing, television distorts the line between fantasy and reality, making it hard for children without an adult nearby (or one on the screen) to explain the difference between what's real and what isn't.

A Window to the World?

Children think of the television set in their homes much the same way they think of the other things that their parents provide, like food and furniture and clothing. Those things, in their own ways, express the parents' values. Whatever a child sees at home carries with it the sense that it's condoned by the parent who provides it and therefore reflects the parents' values.

While some children aren't interested in watching television, many seem to be mesmerized by it and "drink in" whatever they see and hear. Watching television is an intense experience for them, like the way an infant looks at the mother's face while being fed. Television may well have its roots in that early eating experience. Even older children often curl up in a corner of the couch and suck their fingers or munch on snacks as they watch television.

Most television programs are not appropriate for young children, so it's important for parents to choose programs carefully and not just leave the television set turned on all the time. Many children have been frightened by something they've seen on television. It can take a long while for them to get over seeing scary-looking creatures that they fear may get "out of the box!"

Violence on TV

It's an exceedingly important time in the lives of young children when they're working on managing their own aggression and beginning to develop self-control. If they spend hour after hour watching a world where people routinely lose their self-control, our children are seeing over and over again that people are naturally violent. Even when children are watching a program with a message like "crime doesn't pay," they could miss the main idea because of all the attending violence.

Parents Need to Choose TV Carefully

There are so many television channels, children's programs, and videos that it's now harder than ever for parents to know what programs and how much viewing is appropriate. Figuring out how much television is okay to watch is a little like making sure that our children have balanced diets. The best television programming can be a nourishing part

"**M**ister Rogers! How did you get out of the box?"

That's what a young boy asked when he met me. I told him that I'm a real person and that I live in a real home with my family, not in the television. He nodded all through my explanation, and then he asked, "But how are you going to get back into the box?"

Children have so many misconceptions about television that we can't ever take for granted that they really understand what they're watching. Our conversations with them about television let children know that their questions are important and that we care about whatever they're wondering. That gives them clear messages that we're proud of them for the important work they're doing of trying to make sense of the world.

of a complete diet that includes times with parents and with other children, times of active play, times of quiet play, and of course, plenty of time for sleep.

At its best, television can help children feel good about who they are and who they can become. It can stimulate their curiosity, expose them to the arts, and let them see how people and animals behave in naturally healthy ways. Television can also give children and adults a way to "wind down" after a busy day.

Many parents have told us that they choose our *Neighborhood* program for their children because they feel that what we're offering reinforces the things they value in their families, things like kindness, appreciation, curiosity, helping, respect for others, positive problem-solving, self-control, and constructive ways of dealing with feelings. Our *Neighborhood* is deliberately slow-paced so children have time to digest and reflect on what they see and hear.

Most parents try to be careful not to let their children watch programs that are unsuitable for them. But even though we may monitor what our children watch, there's no way to insulate them completely.

One of the most constructive ways parents can handle television is to help their children become critical viewers by encouraging questions and asking them about what they've seen and heard. You might even ask them what they think is real or pretend. In this way, you can help them to become active thinkers rather than people who passively swallow whatever is broadcast.

Create a Dialogue

It can be especially important for parents to talk about cartoons, which can be puzzling for children. A cartoon character may be able to go through a wall or be smashed flat by a steamroller and pop right up again. Even though it's hard for children to

understand that animation is a series of pictures or computer drawings, they need to know that what happens in cartoons is not real life.

We can also help children make sense of commercials. To a child, an "ad" is not much different from a program—it's just shorter, probably faster paced, and has a lot of music. Children need to learn that the purpose of an "ad" is to make people want to buy something. You might want to let your child know that despite the messages they're being shown in commercials, it's *people* who matter most in this world, not toys or clothes or any other possessions.

As long as children have caring adults at hand who want to help them, they can learn to deal with many things in life, including the mixed messages of television. Talking about what they've seen (as well as turning off whatever you feel is inappropriate for your child) is the best way to keep violence or any scary things on TV from becoming overwhelming.

What children get from their parents will always be more important than what TV gives to them. Children who are loved and who feel they are lovable are the ones who will most likely grow into loving, rather than violent, adults. Taking the time to help our children understand themselves, what they see on TV, and their place in the world is another way of showing our love for them. It's another way of letting them know they are protected, unique, and valuable.

Helpful Hints

■ Carefully choose the programs that you feel are suitable for your child. It is a good idea to watch at least one episode of a series with your child so that you'll have some idea of how your child reacts to the program, who the characters are, and what the story is generally about.

■ Make it clear that certain programs or channels are off-limits. Be sure to let babysitters or other caregivers in your home know about the programs or channels you don't want your child to watch. You may even want to mention those things to the parents of your child's playmates.

■ Some families have rules like "No TV when a friend is over," or "No TV after dinner." Rules help children know what's important in their family and can reduce the conflicts about television watching. Knowing the television will be off when a friend comes to play or before bedtime also lets children know that you value their play.

■ When a program is over, turn the television off. Even as background noise, it's highly stimulating, distracting, and interferes with the quiet time that children need for thinking, playing, and using their imagination.

■ Whenever you can, watch television with your child. Being there can give you the opportunity to see how your child reacts, as well as to explain any possible misunderstandings and reinforce whatever positive messages there may be.

■ Let your child know that it's okay to turn off the television if something scary comes on. In fact, being able to turn off a program that's scary is a sign that a child is growing. It takes a brave child to turn off a scary television program!

■ Encourage your child to expand on what was shown on a program by doing an activity from it or making up stories about its characters. The best "use" of television happens when the program is over, the set is turned off, and families use what they've seen in their own unique ways.

Disabilities

"Our son was excited at first about being invited to play at his friend's house, but a few days after the invitation, he refused to go. He told me he was scared of the friend's older brother, who has some kind of disability. Our son said, 'He can't walk and makes scary sounds.' I decided to call the boy's mother, and she was really helpful. She told us about her son's disability and answered some of our questions. I was relieved, and our son seemed to feel better about the play date, too, after we talked with her."

Helping our children feel comfortable with people who have disabilities begins with helping our children feel good about their own uniqueness. When we show them that we love them for all of who they are, regardless of what they can and cannot do, they're more likely to grow up to be adults who accept others just as *they* are.

Alike and Different

Preschoolers are just beginning to be exposed to differences as they expand their interests to other people beyond the family. They're trying to make sense of the world by organizing things into categories. That's why they often become fascinated with matching and sorting games—games about what's alike and what's different.

They tend to categorize *people* that way, too. In their attempt to understand the world, their early categories can be quite rigid: old and young, light-skinned and dark-skinned, girls and boys, good and bad.

That's often why they may want to befriend children who are like them and feel uncomfortable with children who look and sound different from them. Also, a child can sense that adults are uncomfortable when they say something like "don't stare" or when they walk quickly by someone who looks different.

"Can that happen to me?"

Some differences can be particularly upsetting. Since young children don't know much about cause and effect, they can have many misconceptions about their own bodies. They may think that since a stuffed animal's leg can come off, maybe their leg could come off, too. They sometimes might even wonder if they could "catch" a disability by touching someone who has a disability or even by sitting in a wheelchair. They can be particularly fearful of older children and adults who cannot walk. After spending so much effort in recently learning to walk themselves, they may worry that they'll "forget" how to do it someday.

At this time in their lives, children focus a lot on what's "good" and what's "bad." They may wonder if a disability happens as a punishment for doing something "bad," if a person becomes blind from seeing something "bad" or deaf from hearing something "bad." And of course, young children might be afraid that something similar could happen to them as they struggle to control their "bad" urges.

If those kinds of concerns aren't mentioned, they can easily turn into awkwardness, tension, and even fear. But when we encourage children to talk about whatever they're wondering, we often find that they become more accepting and empathetic. Asking and openly talking about differences helps children get beyond the

When Chrissie Thompson first came to work on our television program as the eight-year-old granddaughter of Mrs. and Mr. McFeely (the "Speedy Delivery" people on our program), I found myself being awkward with Chrissie and often minimizing or denying her physical disability. She has spina bifida and has some paralysis in her lower body.

With help from her family and from others in the studio that day, and from Chrissie herself who accepted me just as I was, I finally grew to realize that one of the best things I can do when I meet someone with an obvious physical disability is to acknowledge that disability early on in our relationship. I try not to let much time go by before asking questions about it, like "Were you blind at birth or later?" or "Did you always have to use a wheelchair?" That seems to clear the obstacles and open the way for us to accept every part of each other just as we are.

fears so that they can feel more comfortable with people who have disabilities. As unique as each one of us is, we human beings are much more similar than we are different. That may be the most essential message of all, as we help our children grow towards being caring, compassionate adults.

Attitudes Are Caught, Not Taught

Children take their cues from the adults they love. There's an old Quaker saying that "Attitudes are caught, not taught." We help our children respect others in subtle ways—by the way we adults greet people, talk with them, and talk about them afterwards. Children learn from our example.

Because of the misconceptions and fears that young children have about disabilities, parents need to encourage their children to ask questions, but parents need to be listeners, too. If your child has a question about a disability that you can't answer, you can say, "I don't know, but maybe we can find out." You could ask a person who has the disability to help you with your answer.

Most people like to know you're interested in them. Of course, sensitive parents can help their children learn where, when, and how it's appropriate to ask their questions. Your children may feel more comfortable talking about such things with someone they know well, like an elderly family member or a neighbor.

Certainly children don't have to like everyone in the world. No one does. But with the help of the grownups in their lives, they can learn to be "neighborly": respectful, courteous, and kind. As children grow, they come to understand that if they take the time to get to know someone, they'll discover so much more about that person than what they thought at first.

Helpful Hints

■ When you're talking about someone with a disability, be sure to talk about that person's abilities as well.

■ If you see someone with a disability who might need help, it's a good idea to ask if that person *wants* help. You could talk with your child about times when you or your child appreciated someone's help — and other times when you wanted to do something yourself.

■ Point out things that make it easier for people who have disabilities to manage, like ramps for wheelchairs, Braille signs on elevators, and special computers for people who have difficulty talking.

■ Tell your child about a time when you grew to appreciate someone who seemed different at first. Children need to know that it often takes time to get to know someone and to feel comfortable with that person.

■ Ask your child to talk about what it feels like to come into a group and be ignored or left out. Talking about those feelings can eventually help your child develop empathy for someone with a disability who might feel left out.

■ When you're at the library, look for books about diversity. There are many stories about the ways that people are different. You're helping your child know that diversity is part of what makes this world a rich and interesting place.

■ Talk with your children about things they themselves are able and unable to do. Everyone in the world has abilities *and* disabilities.

Fears

"When we'd go for a walk in our neighborhood, my son was always scared of the barking dog down the street, even though there was a fence keeping the dog in. My first response was to say, 'Oh, don't let it worry you. He can't get out.' I thought it would help him if I could show that there was no way that the dog could get out. But that just didn't help. I finally realized that it wasn't a rational fear, so now I just suggest that we cross the street and I say something like, 'I know that sometimes you're scared of that dog. I'll just hold your hand.'"

The preschool years are years of intense feelings, but most children aren't yet able to use words well enough to express those feelings. Many things can be scary to them—things that are both real and imaginary—and, like all of us, they carry their own "inner dramas" which color everything they see and do. So it's natural that not all children develop the same fears, and that some children are more fearful than others.

Where Children's Fears Might Come From

Children are most often afraid of things that actually *do* what they themselves are trying *not* to do. For instance, when children are trying to master the urge to bite they can become very frightened of things that represent biting, like barking dogs, alligator puppets with big teeth, even pliers, nutcrackers, or still pictures of wild animals in a book.

Such fears might also grow out of children's struggles with their own angry feelings at their parents for making rules and setting limits, paying more attention to a new baby than to them, or for not giving them something they really want. Children can be afraid of getting too angry at their parents because they wonder if maybe their anger could result in losing their parents' love, and that would be devastating. They sometimes project those angry feelings onto some outside thing—a dog, a tiger, a vacuum cleaner, or a toilet drain—and then they fear that the very "angry" thing might just destroy them. Most fears like that tend to calm over time, especially as children realize that a parent can be both loving and angry, and that they themselves can have both loving and angry feelings toward their parents.

The Magic Years

Preschool years are also "magic" years, when children think that things happen by magic, wishing, or pretending. Children don't yet know the difference between what's real and what's pretend. Monsters, ghosts, and nightmares can seem very real, as can scary-looking cartoon or puppet characters in movies or on computers or television.

Because children don't understand how machines work compared to how bodies work, they might think that things like vacuum cleaners, lawn mowers, and heavy construction equipment have lives of their own and could uncontrollably gobble up everything—even children! Children might also worry, "If a doll's arm breaks off, that might happen to my arm!" Even when a mother looks different because of a new hairstyle or different glasses, a child could be scared that she might have

A mother wrote to tell us how her son managed to conquer his fear of the monsters in his nightmares. "The morning after a bad dream, I'd have him describe the monster's scary face and then draw it on a mask that he made on a paper bag. Then he'd chase me around while we laughed and treated the whole thing as a big joke. At the end of the game, we would ceremoniously tear up the mask and stuff it in the garbage can. I told him that the dream was as pretend as the paper mask. After a few of those mask games, his nightmares disappeared. I was relieved—and so was he!"

changed into an entirely different person. In fact, sometimes young children wonder if just putting on a mask or costume might change them into someone different.

One of the most important ways to work on such fears is through their play. When children play about something that's scary for them, they are in charge. They don't have to feel small, helpless, and scared. Each time children play about something, they understand it a little bit better, and they're able to grow a little bit stronger and less afraid.

Parents Can Help Children Feel Safe

Parents want their children to be afraid of some things, because fears can keep children from doing dangerous things. But we don't want our children to develop irrational fears that hold them back from doing healthy things, sleeping well, and making friends.

Part of our "job" as parents is to help our children feel safe and secure. Sometimes it can be very frustrating to try to explain to a frightened child that a monster or witch or some other imaginary thing isn't real. We adults have already learned that, but our children are just beginning.

If you can remember some things you were afraid of when you were a child, you know what it feels like to be scared. Thinking about your own childhood fears helps you to be more in touch with your fearful child and also assures you that, at some point, children can outgrow those fears.

There are many times in life when we can't solve our children's problems or get rid of their fears. Perhaps all we can do is to provide a safe, loving home and a willingness to listen while our children work through whatever is bothering them. "Being there" is often the most active and helpful kind of support parents can give.

Helpful Hints

■ It can help children to know they're not alone in being afraid. Let your child know that many children (and even adults) are afraid of things, even if they don't show it.

■ Listen with care when your child tells you what he or she is afraid of. It doesn't help to tease or to say "There's nothing to be scared of." Fears are real to children. It's important not to discount their feelings.

■ You might want to say something like, "There really aren't any tigers out there, but I understand that you're scared and I'll be here to keep you safe." With reassurance like that, your child may feel strong enough to deal with the fearsome tiger and eventually "tame" it.

■ It's wise to stay away from things that scare your child. You could put away a toy or book that your child finds frightening, and keep the television off if you know there's something scary in the news or other programs.

■ Try not to force your child to do something that is scary. Forcing can make children even more afraid. Children need adults' patient help until they can get over their fear.

■ Give your child something to do, like yelling "Boom!" when the thunder sounds, or turning on a nightlight or flashlight when the bedroom feels too dark. Even pressing the button to turn off a television show when it gets too scary can give your child a sense of power over the fear.

■ It often helps for children to draw a picture or make up a story about a particular "monster" or scary dream. When children can get the scary thing outside of themselves, whether in spoken words or drawn on paper, they're often better able to manage their fears. Getting some distance from the fear makes it easier for children to have some control over it so that it doesn't control them. Of course, even playing or drawing about something can be too scary for some children.

■ Ask a librarian for books that can help children deal with fears. Your child may be able to hear about something scary if it's in a book—and if you are nearby.

■ Some families give their children a spray bottle with water as "monster spray," or put a sign on the door that says "No monsters allowed." That may seem to work in the short term because children are so trusting and willing to believe the fantasy, but what it could say to them is that their parents, too, think that monsters are real, and that the monsters might actually be there. In the long term, we want them to know that monsters aren't real and that they really are not there.

■ If you're concerned that you'll "transfer" your own fears to your child, you could ask someone else to help in certain situations. For example, if a mother has a great fear of the dentist, the father, an aunt, or a close cousin could be the one to take a child to the dentist.

Brothers and Sisters

"When my children got into fights with each other, I used to listen to both sides and try to be fair in judging who was right and who was wrong. But the fights didn't stop, and I realized that I was probably making things worse by trying to be a referee. When the two of them argue now, I get them to figure out a solution themselves. They aren't always able to do that, but they don't ask me to jump in as often. I think they're getting better about solving their own conflicts."

Brothers and sisters

shape a child's early experiences almost as much as parents do. In the everyday ups and downs of family life, children learn about getting along with those who have different perspectives and different abilities. Living through each day, they come to understand something essential about love: there can be times of impatience as well as kindness, disappointment as well as thoughtfulness, anger as well as forgiveness. Even though brothers and sisters may fight and disagree, they have a unique connection.

Sharing Parents' Love

It's right in the family that children encounter their first intense competition, especially between the first born and the baby brother or sister. Even older children who are secure in their family may have ambivalent feelings about the new baby. Anybody would like to be his or her parents' "one and only" loved child, but giving that up can be an enormous boost in growing. And, of course, it allows the older child to discover first hand the joys of being a brother or sister.

Different Ages, Different Interests

Because competition is so much a part of the relationship between the first and second child, those two children particularly may have a lot of conflicts. Many of those conflicts happen because younger children idolize their older brothers and sisters and want so much to be a part of their play. But their age differences, with their different abilities and needs, sometimes make playing together really hard, if not impossible. The older child is excited about learning and mastering new things and is not very concerned with the things that matter to the younger child. The younger child often hasn't the slightest idea what the older brother or sister wants or needs. It can take a long time before they're able to play well together, and even then, they may have quite different interests.

Most families find that competition lessens as their children get older and become involved in activities outside the home, when they aren't so dependent on their parents for approval and recognition. The competition also tends to ease when children know that we parents see each one of our children as a unique individual, without comparing or making them follow in each other's footsteps. When our children sense that we value each one's gifts, talents, and ideas, then they're more likely to grow into people who have that kind of respect for each other.

Parents' Expectations

When parents bring another baby into the family, they can be concerned about the

A mother of a three-year-old son and one-year-old twins told me that her oldest son was getting rough with his little brothers. She often had to stop him from hurting them. Soon it dawned on her that whenever he was being friendly, she left him alone, but when he was aggressive, he got her full attention. She started to devote special times for just her and her firstborn, and she began to look for moments to compliment him when he was being cooperative. With that kind of attention from her, he was able to manage much better his times with his brothers.

challenges of caring for and loving another child. But they can also feel there's something very special about giving their older child (or children) a "gift" of a lifetime friend who shares the family history. Our expectations and fantasies about that probably have a lot to do with our own growing up, with or without brothers and sisters.

Parents are often disappointed when their children aren't "good buddies," but in most families it takes a long time for brothers and sisters to work through their competition for their parents' attention. It can also take a great deal of work to help the older ones learn to be understanding and patient with the younger ones, and the younger ones to be considerate of the older ones.

Mediating Conflicts

Children sometimes try to draw their parents into their squabbles. Each one wants to hear you say, "You're the good one"—the favorite—and make the other "the bad one"—the outcast. Rather than judging who's right and who's wrong, it's better to help children learn to listen to each other (without interrupting) and work together to settle their own conflicts. It's helpful for parents to say, "I know you both want to play with the same thing. Let's think of some ways to work it out." It's best not to take sides, place blame, or focus on what caused the problem. Being able to resolve conflicts peacefully is one of the greatest strengths we can give our children—now and for the rest of their lives.

I'm the BIG brother

Each Child Is Unique

It's only natural that a parent will be more in tune with one (or some) of his or her children than others, maybe because of the child's temperament, interests, gender, or birth order. Because parents sometimes feel guilty about having that kind of connection with one of their children, they may overcompensate with the others, giving them more attention or being more lenient with them. Children can sense when there's something unnatural like that going on with their parents, and that can make them feel uneasy. If parents understand that it's perfectly normal to feel more in tune with one child than another, they may be able to put their guilt aside so that it won't get in the way when they're trying to be fair with each of their children.

And it's fairness among our children that we want to achieve—not equality. It isn't fair to treat children *equally* if they have different abilities, needs, and interests. If one child needs—and gets—more help, attention, or comfort from us, the others will sense that we'll be there for them, too, when they need us. And through our example, our children are more likely to be sensitive when a brother or sister is in need of extra support. Being there for each other, through the good times and the bad, is the best "gift" that we're helping the brothers and sisters give to each other.

Helpful Hints

■ Make sure your children have some time away from each other. Let them know it's even okay to say something like, "I can't play with you now, but I will later" (but be sure they keep that promise of coming back later to play). If you make children include their brothers or sisters too much of the time, they can grow to be resentful.

■ Encourage your children to do something together that's non-competitive and creative, like making paper chains or playing with play clay or art materials. Let them know that you value the uniqueness of what each of them can do.

■ Try your best to give each child some of your undivided attention—perhaps at bedtime, when a younger child naps, after dinner, or on the weekend. When children know they can count on having some time with you all by themselves, they may be better able to manage when you can't give them your full attention.

■ If possible, make different bedtimes for your children so that each can have some one-on-one time with you before going to sleep. That's a very important time for saying, "I love you" to each child.

■ Many families find that conflicts decrease if the older children know there are some things they do not have to share. Those things can be put out of reach of the younger ones. If there are some things children don't ever have to share, they're often more willing to share other things.

■ When one child has a friend over for play, it's important not to insist that they include a brother or sister in their play. Find something you can do with your other child, like working on a meal together, reading a book, or asking that child to play near you.

■ If you know another family with children about the same age as yours, see if the two older ones can play together in one home, while the two younger ones are at the other home. Being apart with different friends for some of the time can help brothers and sisters manage better when they are together.

Pets

"Our daughter was snapping her fingers in front of our dog's face. It was just playful teasing, but I asked her not to do it and told her that it makes the dog feel bad. She seemed so surprised and said to me, 'I didn't know dogs had feelings!'"

For a child, a pet can be a trusted friend who gives unconditional love, a companion when no one else will play, a smaller creature over whom children have some control, and a comforter on difficult days. A pet can also help children learn about discipline and responsibility, about new life and even death.

Challenges of Caring for a Pet

Young children aren't able to handle much of the responsibility that's involved in caring for a pet. They even have to be reminded of their own routines, like washing their hands before eating or brushing their teeth before going to bed. Nevertheless, it is possible that through time a pet can help a child learn to be a responsible caregiver.

We can't expect young children to be naturally gentle and caring with a pet. To them, a pet is at first like a toy. Out of curiosity, they might hold the pet upside down, lift a floppy ear to see what's underneath, step on a tail, or try to ride a dog like a pony. Preschoolers don't see things from

> *When I was little and didn't have a sister yet, I had a dog named Mitzi. She was a brown, wire-haired mongrel, and for a long time, I think she really was my best friend. In each other's company we learned a lot about the world. We explored our neighborhood and beyond. I remember being a little braver whenever Mitzi was with me. We shared excitement, joy, and sadness. We got scared together in thunderstorms. After Mitzi died, I was very sad.*
>
> *My parents knew it would be "good for me" to have a dog for a companion. Well, it was good for me. Her life and her unique love will always be a part of who I am. I'm so grateful to have "grown up" with her.*

someone else's point of view. They may not even realize that a pet is a living creature.

Learning to Respect Animals

Some young children might think that there's a little person inside the pet, and treat it as such. Animals are often given human qualities in children's books, television, movies, and puppetry, where animals talk, wear clothes, and even sing and dance! In fact, it's often through stuffed animals and picture books that the relationship between children

and animals begins. But children soon find that real animals wiggle out of baby carriages and don't tolerate being dressed up in doll clothes. That's when children learn that a pet is an animal who is to be treated like all other living creatures—with gentleness and respect.

Parents and Pets

Parents must be partners with their children in sharing the work of feeding, caring for, and cleaning up after a pet. We need to make sure children don't get overburdened by a responsibility they may not be ready for yet.

Parents need to help protect the pets, too. Young children can't be expected to know what to do about beaks and claws and teeth, and animals can't be expected to know what to do about hair pulling and squeezing.

What Children Can Learn from a Pet

When we explain to our children the limits we give to our pets, such as where and how it's okay to play, our children can better understand why we make limits for them as well—for health, safety, and for having some order in family life. When pets ignore those limits, children see us parents scold and make restrictions on the pet. In fact, many parents have overheard their children scolding a dog or cat for running out of the yard, in the same tone the adults have used! At times like that, children seem to be growing in their understanding that limits are expressions of affection.

No one can predict exactly what changes will take place when a pet joins a family, but it's fairly certain that changes will happen—some of them pleasant and others maybe not so pleasant. While pets generally add more complications to a household, they also add an enriching dimension to the many layers of caring and confirmation of family life.

Helpful Hints

Bringing a Pet into the Family:

■ You may want to consider starting with a small pet, such as a fish, a bird, a gerbil, a hamster, a turtle, or a guinea pig. Caring for those pets is not terribly demanding. Also, that kind of pet is mostly for watching rather than handling, so with them children can begin to learn about animals in a simple way.

■ Before you bring a pet home, you might want to help your child practice "gentle touching" by stroking a stuffed animal. Remember that young children are impulsive and they're just learning to control their hands and legs, so you may have to give a number of reminders about "gentle touch."

■ When a little pet is scurrying around or your cat is meowing or the dog is barking, you might ask your child, "What do you think he (or she) wants?" That can help your child think of the pet as a creature with needs and feelings and begin to respond with compassion.

When a Pet Dies:

■ The death of a pet reminds us all, young and old, that sad things happen in life. It's natural to miss a beloved pet, and to cry, no matter how old we are.

■ Everyone in the family has special memories and a unique relationship with the pet, and each one has his or her own unique way of dealing with the death. Encourage your child to talk about the pet's death so you can better understand what such a loss means to your child.

■ Whatever we can talk about can be far more manageable than if we don't talk about it. Also, looking at photos and talking about memories can help children know there are ways to keep their pet "alive" in their hearts.

■ Playing with a stuffed animal can give children a way to express their feelings and find comfort when a beloved pet dies. They might pretend to make their pet come alive again. In children's pretend play, they can be in control of what happens. Their drawings can help in that way, too.

■ Give your child time to grieve. Understanding what death means will come little by little. It often takes some time for a child to be ready to accept a "replacement."

■ While much about death is a mystery, there are some things children can understand. For instance, we can tell them things like "When a pet dies, it doesn't need to eat, it can't see or hear, it isn't breathing and moving anymore— and it won't come to life again."

■ Children are quite literal, and they can be terribly afraid to go to sleep at night if they've heard about a pet "being put to sleep." They need to know that death is *not* like a daytime rest or a nighttime sleep.

■ Children may think a pet died as a punishment for being "bad." It's important for them to hear that all pets and all children do "bad" things now and then. They also need to know that it wasn't anything they did that made the pet die—and they cannot make it come back to life again.

■ Many families find it helpful to have a funeral for the pet. Just being together, sharing thoughts and feelings with family and friends, can begin to make children feel better and help them to remember the happy times with their pet.

Making Friends

"Our daughter was so glad to find out that the new family moving in next door had a girl her age. She and the new neighbor became 'best friends.' But just when the two girls seemed to be playing together well, they'd get into a fight over a toy or something they were playing about. One of them would stomp away and yell, 'You're not my friend any more!' The other would say, 'And I'm not inviting you here ever again!' At first I was tempted to jump in and fix things, but before long those two girls were 'best friends' again!"

One of life's greatest joys is the comfortable give and take of a good friendship. It's a wonderful feeling not only to have a friend, but to know how to be a friend yourself.

Early Friendships

Some children are naturally sociable, and from early on seem to love to have playmates. Other children are more private and seem content to do things by themselves. Not wanting to play with others or clinging to a parent may be their way of saying, "Instead of getting to know those other people right now, what I need is more time to get to know me!"

Many young children aren't ready yet for certain kinds of sociability.

When children do make their first social connection, it's usually *side by side*. They might play next to each other in the same area or with similar playthings. They may just watch each other or imitate each other. That's how friendship begins—with the understanding that "you're someone else and I'm someone else."

"My Best Friend"

The ability to play *with* another child comes later, along with the growing delight (and

> *A* mother told us that her son liked to invite friends over to play, but soon after a friend arrived, an explosion would erupt between the two. It seemed that her son had a really hard time sharing his toys—he was furious if a friend wanted to play with his things. His mother suggested that he put away a few toys that weren't to be shared. With a few chosen toys safely put away, her son was better able to get along with his playmate. It seemed that just knowing there were some toys that he didn't have to share helped him be able to share the others.

frustration) of sharing ideas. Friendships become "give and take," filled with ups and downs, as children learn to compromise, cooperate, and work through differences in feelings and styles.

Those early friendships tend to be temporary—"of the moment." When a child refers to someone as "my friend," that usually means "we're playing together right now." Being named "my friend"—or better still, "my best friend"—is so important to children that when things aren't going well, the most powerful threat they can think of is, "You are not my friend any more." That's usually just their way of saying, "I'm really angry that you won't go along with my ideas." The conflict is often forgotten after a short time, and the two friends are back together again.

The Work of Friendships

Young children have much to learn about sharing toys and sharing ideas and that kind of learning happens over a long period of time. It takes years for young children to begin to see things from someone else's point of view, and to learn about managing all those complicated feelings that come with friendships, like anger, love, disappointment, frustration, and jealousy.

When young friends have a chance to deal with those feelings, they can often learn that an important part of friendship is working things out after a disagreement and finding that their relationship is even stronger than before.

Parents Value Friendships

Our culture places a high value on friendships and on being "popular." And of course, parents want their children to have friends because they feel they'll have happier times in school and a more confident, interesting life beyond school. No wonder we adults are concerned about our children's ability to make friends!

Understanding Children's Friendships

Some parents may have wonderful memories of childhood friendships, while others remember feeling like outsiders and longing for friends. Through our lives most of us have had a variety of social experiences. If we can remember those different kinds of friendships that we've had through the years, we can better understand that our children probably will, too.

What a delight it can be for parents when their child plays well with a friend! But it can be equally disheartening to watch your child fight with a friend over a toy or to have to take the friend home early when a playdate ends in unresolved conflict. Learning to share and learning to compromise are enormous challenges for young children, whose view of the world is still quite self-centered.

Should I Intervene?

When children fight, they need their parents to step in to help them find healthy solutions, but they also need parents to be patient and to have realistic expectations. Many parents are surprised to find that their children's conflicts are momentary and temporary. The next day the children may have forgotten the problem completely, and the two children will be "best friends" once again—without any intervention.

Sometimes parents feel they need to be "referees," but it can be far more effective to be "mediators," helping children hear each other's point of view and helping them find a workable solution. If children aren't able to make up again after the disruptions and explosions, they may need some extra help from parents, even when things have calmed down. Some young children stay mad a long time, and they don't have the skills to rebuild a friendship. Those children need their parents to help them talk things out, so they can remember the good times they have had with their friend.

The biggest help we give our children is the examples we set in our own friendships. Attitudes are "caught" more than "taught." That's true for empathy and tolerance and all the other things that have to do with being a good friend. It is from us and our everyday attitudes that our children are likely to learn the most.

Alone-Time Is Important

Sometimes preschoolers seem to be "loners." They just don't want to play with other children. To some adults that doesn't seem natural; however, it may be both natural and necessary. Since many children these days spend a lot of time in group care, solitude may be just what they need most when they get home.

Until a child has developed a reasonably secure sense of self, playing with other children can quickly become over-stimulating. Self-confidence grows best when children have time alone or in the company of loved and trusted adults. It's through their early closeness with their primary caregivers that children grow to be social.

Helpful Hints

■ The first playdate between two children could be a short get-together, like a picnic or snack. The two children might make something simple together for the meal. It can take a while for some children to feel comfortable at an unfamiliar home, and so you may want to invite the child's parent, too.

■ When a friend comes to play, suggest activities that are less likely to create conflict, like making a long paper chain or playing with things that are easily shared, like play clay, blocks, craft materials, construction paper, crayons, and paints.

■ You might want to stay nearby or at least within ear range when new friends are playing together. Children's conflicts can erupt suddenly, and it helps if you can step in early. Just your being nearby will probably keep the players' "comfort level" high.

■ When there are disagreements, let the children know that you understand that sometimes friends just don't agree on certain things. Even people who like each other a lot can agree to disagree. Encourage the children to think of ways to work things out so that neither one loses. Learning to come to a mutual "win-win" resolution will serve them all their lives.

■ If you can remember a time when you and a childhood (or adult) friend disagreed or had a dispute, tell your child how you worked things out. It helps children to hear that their parents have had to work hard at resolving conflicts, too. That shows them what value you give to maintaining good friendships.

Learning Readiness

"Everyone said it was important to read to my child, so I brought out the usual children's picture books. My four-year-old son wouldn't sit and listen to them—the only thing he was interested in was hockey. His preschool teacher suggested that I look for a book about hockey players, so I went to the library and brought home one about his favorite player. I started to read to him, and he wouldn't let me stop! We finished a whole chapter that afternoon, and he wanted me to keep on reading!"

Children are born ready to learn. Right from the start, they begin learning about the world through touch, smell, sounds, and sight. All through the early years, that's how they learn best—through their primary senses. They put things together, move them around, experiment, explore, and discover.

Learning through Play

While children may look like they're "just playing," they are also working on some of the basic things they'll need in order to be able to read, write, and do math later on. What's more, they're learning about those things in a way that's natural and interesting for them.

"More and less," "different and same," "top and bottom"—these are some of the basic concepts children need to understand to be ready for learning about letters and numbers in school. When children play and pretend, they're learning those kinds of things

in ways that are meaningful to them—much more meaningful than if they're just given fragmented bits of information (like 1+1=2) to which they can't relate. When children make mud pies and need "more" water for the right consistency, or need "one more" spoon for the pretend party so each stuffed animal can have its own, "more" as a math concept has real meaning.

In those kinds of everyday ways, children develop one of the most essential tools for school readiness—a sense that the world is an interesting place. They can be fascinated by the simplest things they see and hear, even taking a long time to look closely at a bug crawling up a tree trunk or a crack in the sidewalk.

The "Tools" for Learning

To be ready and eager for school learning, children don't need fancy, expensive, "educational" toys. What they do need is to feel good about who they are and what they can do. They also need to be able to stick to a task, deal with their mistakes, use their imagination, accept rules and limits, be curious about the world around them, and get along with others. Those are the readiness "tools" that will help them be successful learners in the classroom and beyond.

When we give children opportunities to play, we're giving them hands-on ways to develop those tools for learning. For instance, when

> *A mother wrote to tell us that her daughter wears her down with her constant string of "why's." She told us that if she senses it's a "why" that her daughter really wants to know about, she almost always gives her an answer, but sometimes she feels "why" becomes a game. So she made up a short song—"Whys are great, they help us learn, sometimes they make mommy impatient." What a great way to show her daughter she respected her curiosity and at the same time let her know that mothers have limits, too!*

they put their time and energies into building something from blocks and it accidentally knocks down, or they're drawing a picture that doesn't turn out the way they expected, they can learn about how to handle frustration and disappointment. If they decide to rebuild the structure or to make another drawing, they're learning about persistence.

Young children aren't yet able to share or to work things out when they come up against differences of opinions. If we think of their conflicts as teachable moments, we can help them grow in their ability to listen and to see things from another person's perspective. What happens in a classroom isn't just between teacher and students, it's also among the children.

In any classroom there are bound to be disagreements, angry moments, and hurt feelings. If children come to school knowing how to get along with others and having healthy ways to express their feelings—especially their frustration—they'll be much better able to handle the day-to-day ups and downs in the classroom.

Of course, children develop these "tools" from the examples their parents set for them. Children want to be like the people they love. It's important for them to see that we adults sometimes have problems, but we work on solving them constructively; that we have trouble learning certain things, but we keep on trying to learn; that now and then we have conflicts with other family members or friends, but we do our best to get along with them. Attitudes are contagious!

Parents' Expectations

Parents want their children to be good learners and to do well in school, but the pressure for that kind of success seems to be starting earlier and earlier. It's hard to know how much to "push" learning in the early years and how much to trust that children will learn on their own. When children's inner rhythm tells them they're ready, most children will learn reading and math—just the way they naturally learned to crawl by following their own inner timetable.

If we pressure children to learn something before they're ready, they can become anxious, frustrated, and angry, and that can affect their feelings about all kinds of learning. There's a world of difference between *insisting* on someone's doing something and establishing an atmosphere in which that person can grow into *wanting* to do it.

The first things children usually want to learn about are the things they care most about: writing their own name, the word "love," and the names of the people they care most about—"mom" and "dad"—are often their first handwritten treasures. Learning and loving go hand in hand, in many, many ways.

Showing a genuine appreciation for the things our children make, talk about, and play about is by all means the best climate for learning. When we listen—really listen— to children's ideas, concerns, and feelings, we're showing them that their words and ideas matter. More importantly, we're showing that they *themselves* matter to us. When children feel good about who they are, they're likely to be eager learners both inside and outside the classroom.

Helpful Hints

■ Talk about things that were hard for you to do when you were a child, like riding a bike or learning to write. You could even share your experiences with things that were difficult for you to master as an adult, like a new computer or phone system. Children are much more likely to stick to a task if they understand that it takes time for *everyone* to learn things.

■ When you talk about a problem that you're dealing with at home or at work, try not to just complain. Let your child hear that you're working on a solution. Even if you can't fix the problem, your child will know that people don't just give up when they're facing something difficult.

■ Give your child responsibilities that he or she can handle. Children need to feel they're successful at some things, even small accomplishments like being able to draw a circle or make a peanut butter sandwich.

■ If your child feels discouraged by a "job" that feels too hard, try breaking the job down into smaller parts. Instead of the huge task of "clean up your room," your child might find it much more manageable if you suggest first putting away the stuffed animals, then the toy cars, then the blocks, etc.

Helping Your Child Appreciate Books and Reading:

■ Set aside warm, close times for reading to your child. The feelings of those times will stay with your child. Later on, just holding a book will remind your child of those pleasant reading times with you.

■ When you're reading a book, give your child opportunities to ask questions and to talk about the story and the pictures. You might want to ask things like, "What do you see in that picture?" or "What do you think will happen next?"

■ It's okay if your child asks for the same book or books over and over again. If children have heard parents read a book again and again, there may come a time when they can "read" it from memory. "Pretend reading" is an important step towards actual reading, and it can help your child feel successful at being able to "read" a book.

Holidays and Birthdays

"By our son's third birthday, my wife and I had already come to the conclusion that 'What do you want for your birthday?' was an unfair question. How could he know what was reasonable to ask for? We felt such an open-ended question just set us all up for trouble. We started making his birthday 'surprise day.' Our son would find a surprise present where he wasn't expecting it: at the breakfast table, under his chair, and at other places during the day. The last two presents were always on his pillow at night, and they were small gifts from his mother and me. During those years that's how we solved the problem of 'too much all at once and over too soon.'"

Some adults create so much excitement about birthdays and holidays that children come to think of them as the most special days of the year. With a focus on family gatherings, presents, and parties, there's a lot for children to look forward to and to fantasize about.

Too Much of a Good Thing?

It's only natural that the heightened anticipation of birthdays and holidays might lead to expectations that can never be met. Unfortunately, when children find that the anticipation is so much greater than the actuality, they can be disappointed, angry, and upset.

Even if expectations are met, it can be hard for a child to receive too much of anything—gifts, food, attention—at any one time. In fact, it can be just plain overwhelming for children to receive so much of everything. They may wonder, "How can I make up for all this? How can I ever say 'thank you' enough? How can I ever be good enough in return for all of this?"

Creating Family Traditions

Almost every family has some traditions for holidays or birthdays—being together at a certain place, making some special holiday food, singing certain songs, lighting candles. Most people say it's those traditions that make the days special for them. Traditions can be like anchors that help us feel more secure and stable. They can be especially important when families feel the frenzy that sometimes comes with the holidays.

Traditions give us a framework for celebrating. But some of those traditions that were comforting for parents in their childhood families may not work well for their children today. Over the years, families tend to develop their own traditions. We may be surprised at how little it takes to make a day feel really special.

Commotion and crowds can be over-stimulating for children and make it harder for them to control their impulses. During long family gatherings, children tend to manage better if they have a place of their own that's safely out of the way of the adults—a place where they can go to do their own kinds of things. It could be a place outside, a quiet room with some books and toys, or just a space behind a sofa in the living room.

Parents Want a "Perfect" Day

Birthdays and other holidays sometimes make parents feel like they're being swept up in a

A young boy once wrote to us after his birthday party. "I'm mad and sad. I didn't want my friends to go home." For him, it wasn't a happy birthday. But his mother gave him a way to handle his disappointment by helping him put his feelings into words—"mad" and "sad." Since he was able to talk about some of the things that upset him, he might have been better able to see that there were other things he did enjoy so his whole birthday wouldn't feel like a complete disappointment.

whirlwind. They're naturally concerned about their over-worrying, overworking, and over-spending! And in the desire to try to make the holiday a perfect day for their children, they can easily be led to enormous disappointment.

In the case of the winter holidays, that desire to create the perfect day is fanned to a great blaze by media. The loudest message of the season, shouted from millions of television sets, newspapers, and magazines, seems to be: "To spend more is to love more, and to be more dearly loved."

What a seductive message, especially for parents! When a baby is born, parents feel that they would like to give their baby a perfect life. But of course that's not realistic, especially if "perfection" means a life that is always happy. Our children will sometimes hurt, have stomachaches and growing pains, feel jealousy and disappointment. Very early in our children's lives we will be forced to realize that the "perfect" (untroubled) life we'd like for them is just a fantasy. Nevertheless, there's a persistent fantasy that "Even if I can't give my child a perfect life, maybe I can at least make a perfect day once or twice each year—on his or her birthday, and at Christmas or Hanukkah or . . ."

Coping with Disappointment

Often the anticipated day brings tears, fights, and disappointments, with parents feeling at the end of the day that their children never appreciated any of it. "We did all of this for you, and why aren't you happy?" There's a letdown that turns that "perfect" day into a big disappointment. Of course, no one wants to disappoint a child; however, an important part of being a parent is helping children cope with disappointment.

Children sometimes ask for gifts their parents can't afford or don't feel are appropriate. We can help children learn early on that there are limits to what people can have. Some parents have told their children, "We can't buy everything you want. We don't have enough money for all that. We need money for our home, food, clothes, and taking care of the other things that you need and we need." If

parents are supportive, they can help a child face disappointment and grow from it. And coping with disappointment is a "gift" that they'll be able to use all their lives.

Celebrate the Small Things

While we generally think of celebrating big occasions, some of the best things to celebrate are the small moments that happen in every day life, like seeing someone help another person, learning something new, or noticing a beautiful sunset, a pretty flower, or a flight of birds. When we can take the time in the midst of our busy world to celebrate things like that, we're nourishing our children and ourselves.

Helpful Hints

For Birthday Parties:

■ For a birthday party, it can help to limit the number of guests to the age of your child—three friends for a three-year-old party; four friends for a four-year-old party. With these limitations, you can probably keep the size of the party down to a number that is comfortable for both you and your child.

■ Figure out some simple ways to celebrate. What matters most is that it be something that your child chooses, which is agreeable to you, and something that the family can do together—like selecting the menu for dinner, going on a picnic, or to the playground.

■ Find other times besides birthdays to celebrate your child's growing, like when your child has helped someone, learned something new, or handled a difficult situation well. "Inside" growing is as important to celebrate as "outside" growing. Some families light a candle or give a special cup or plate to the child who is being honored on these special occasions to create their own family traditions.

For the Winter Holidays:

■ Find some quiet time before the holidays to ask your child what traditions he or she has enjoyed over the years. They may be the ones you want to make sure to preserve.

■ Involve your child in the pre-holiday activities by working together to make name cards for the family meal, making cookies, creating holiday cards, or setting up the candles. Participating gives children an important sense of belonging.

■ Before going to another home for a family gathering for the holidays, let your child know what to expect. Talk about what you know about the house, your memories of being there (if you were there as a child), and the guests who might be there.

■ Try to be aware of when your child *begins* to be stressed and go to a quiet place with your child to lie down for a while, to look at a book, or to take a walk. Once children become over-stimulated, exhausted, fretful, or just plain out of control, it's harder for them to settle down. They need to feel confident that their parents will help them get back into control.

Bedtime

"Our four-year-old started waking up every night and expecting me to sleep with her. I felt sorry for her and stayed with her until she (and I!) fell asleep. After that it was really hard to break the habit. I finally started to believe that sleeping with her wasn't helpful for her or for me. I think she heard in my voice that I was serious, and that she could feel safe in her own room. After a few nights, she found ways to settle herself back to sleep."

Bedtime can be a difficult time. Most children don't like to stop doing something fun to get ready for bed, and they certainly don't like being told when to stop what they're doing. It's only natural that they want to continue being a part of whatever is going on in the family, even at night.

Coping with Separation

Bedtime is especially hard for young children because it means being separated from parents. A child doesn't understand much about time, so it's hard to know how long it takes for morning to come. Young children can't be sure when they'll be back with the people they love.

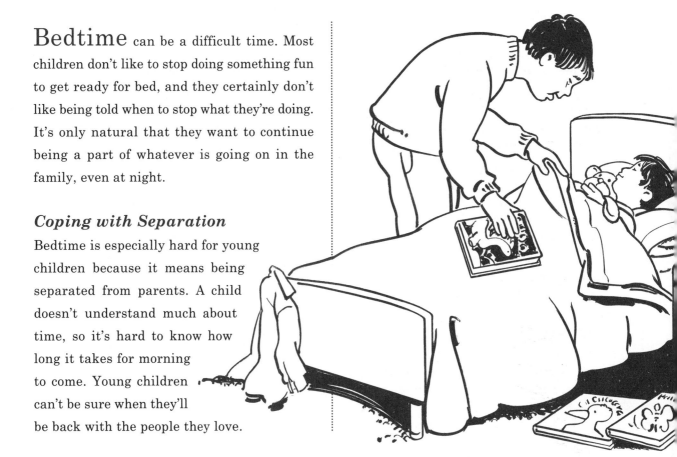

That's why a time of calmness, closeness, and reassurance before bedtime can be really important. Children need to know that their parents or someone else they trust will be nearby when the day turns into night.

Routines Help Children Manage

One of the best ways to deal with bedtime struggles is to set up routines and rules. Children are much more comfortable when they know what to expect and when they know what is expected of them. Consistency and predictability go a long way toward helping children manage their behavior and their feelings at nighttime as well as during the daytime.

Be prepared, though, for children to test the rules that you make. It may take a while for them to see that you're firm about bedtime. In the meantime, you can let them know that even if they don't like the rules, it's important to follow them.

Of course, there are times like holidays, when you have visitors, or when your child is sick that you'll have to change the usual schedule. If you explain why you're changing the routine and that the change is just temporary, your child will know that the usual

A friend told me that her father always made up a story for her and her brothers at bedtime, a story about three little ducks who had a series of different adventures. "You know," she said, "no matter how bad we had been, he never threatened not to tell us that story. There were other consequences, but he never used that evening time with us as a punishment. I certainly didn't think about it then, but now I believe that his continuing stories reassured us that there would be another day coming after the night, and Dad's presence somehow told us that just as life would continue from day to day, so, too, would love."

schedule is still important and that eventually things will be back to normal.

No matter what, there may be some nights when your child might have an especially hard time saying good night. Your child might be overly stimulated, sick, upset by significant changes in the family, or having a difficult time for no reason that's apparent to you. On evenings like that, you might want to spend some extra time with your child before bedtime, sitting beside the bed a little longer than usual, talking, singing softly, giving a hug.

Little by little, children learn that nighttime will come, separation will take place, they will fall asleep, and then daytime will come again and they will wake up safely in their own beds, with the people they love still there to care for them. That security is a wonderful gift for any human being!

Parents Have Needs, Too

No healthy parent likes to end the day with arguments and anger. We want to help our children get to sleep in an atmosphere of warmth and caring—for their sake and for our own.

There probably will be times, however, when your child pleads with you to stay up later. It may seem easier to give in, but it can help to remember that children really do want to know that their parents are in charge and that they will be firm about the rules. When we stick to rules and routines, we're helping our children feel more secure, and therefore more loved.

It's only natural that parents want to settle their children in bed so they can have some time to themselves. Parents need time without the demands of a child's attention—for peace and quiet, for having adult conversation, for doing household chores, working, or studying. When parents have some time for their own needs, they're often better able to nourish their family.

Helpful Hints

Before Bedtime:

■ Bedtime starts long before children are in bed. In fact, children are far more ready for bedtime if they have "winding down" time with some calm, relaxing activities. It's wise to avoid television programs that might make your children excited or feel they need rough and tumble play. If you offer an evening snack, keep away from foods with caffeine, like colas and chocolate, which are stimulants and could keep your child awake. Better to give fruit, pretzels, or a cookie and a little milk.

■ Try to make bedtime the same time each night. Children understand what's expected of them when they have a routine that's predictable.

■ About fifteen minutes before bedtime, and again five minutes before, remind your child that bedtime is coming soon. It's hard for children to stop doing something they enjoy, and a reminder gives them time to finish what they're doing and to get ready to "switch gears" for actual bedtime routines. Some people find it helpful to use neutral timekeepers like clocks or a timer to help children see when it's time for bed.

■ Let your children know that you understand how disappointed they can get when they have to stop playing and get ready for bed. Just knowing that parents care about their feelings can help children manage better.

■ Set up a bedtime routine. Give your child choices. Some families find their children are more willing to go through a bedtime routine if they have some control over what particular things they do. Of course, there are some things, like bathing and teeth brushing, that need to be part of every healthy family's "routine." Below is a list of some other rituals you may want to consider:
    Read books or tell stories
    Give hugs
    Spend time cuddling with a parent
    Sing quiet songs
    Listen to quiet music
    Talk about what happened today and
        what's ahead for tomorrow
    Say prayers
    Say goodnight to things in the room:
        "Goodnight pillow,
        goodnight books . . ."

Helping Your Child Stay in Bed:

■ Find a balance between being comforting and being firm about the rules. If you've set a rule of "one small drink of water" or "two books," kindly remind your child of the rule and then stick to it.

■ Let your child know that it's okay if he or she doesn't fall asleep right away, but that it's important to stay in bed.

■ Encourage your children to find ways to comfort themselves—maybe holding a stuffed animal, making up a story, or imagining a pleasant "dream."

■ Your child might find it comforting to have something of yours to keep through the night, like a glove or a small scarf. Those personal things can help your child feel connected with you, even though you're not right there.

■ If you feel comfortable about it, you may want to leave on a night light or decorate your child's bedroom walls or ceiling with glow-in-the-dark stickers. Having a bit of light reminds children that there is still light somewhere, and that before long the daylight will come again.

■ Some families find it helpful to leave the bedroom door open a bit, so children can hear some familiar sounds of the household as they try to fall asleep.

■ If children do get out of bed, it's best to walk them back to their rooms. Children need to know their own beds and bedrooms are safe places.

■ If your child has had a nightmare, you can assure your child that a dream is only a dream, and a dream can't hurt anybody.

■ Some families put a sticker on a calendar each morning after their child was able to stay in bed all night. There may not be many stickers to begin with, but seeing them increase over time can let children realize that they've been able to manage something that once had been hard for them.

First Experiences

For young children, life is full of new experiences. Some are exciting, others are scary—some are exciting *and* scary! It's hard for parents to know what might be difficult for children to handle or how much help they may need. No matter what, everyone likes to be told what to expect when we're facing something new. The help that we give young children early on can influence the way they approach and cope with new situations all their lives.

Sometimes parents think that if they don't talk about what to expect, they're protecting their children. But when children are put into new experiences without any preparation, they're likely to be even more upset because they're caught off guard. Their fantasies are often much scarier than the reality.

When we talk openly about a new experience—what will probably happen and what probably *won't* happen—children can feel more prepared and better able to manage, and they'll trust us even more. Encouraging them to talk with us about their feelings can be an important step toward helping them manage those feelings.

First experiences are great opportunities for children to grow. They are also times for them to discover how well people of all ages can cope when there is love, trust, and honest communication.

Using the Toilet

"My son seemed to catch on to toilet training right away. For three days he went on the potty and stayed dry at child care! He was proud of himself, and we all made a big fuss. But the next day in child care, he wet his pants twice, and from then on, he insisted on going back to diapers. I was really upset, but some other moms helped me to relax, and I let a few weeks go by. Now and then I mentioned toilet training to my son. It's taken a couple of weeks, but he's now finally talking about trying again."

There's a lot of work involved in learning to use the toilet. Children have to learn to control their muscles to hold on or let go at just the right time. They have to stop doing something they really like and go right away to the bathroom. What's more, they have to learn to let go of something their body produces and have it flushed away down a drain. They may wonder, "If I let go too much, will all of me come out and get flushed down the toilet?" No wonder it's so hard to master toilet training, and no wonder children sometimes wet or soil their pants as they're learning!

Signs of Readiness

Many parents wonder when to begin toilet training with their children. It's best to wait until you feel that your child is "ready." Children often give signs of readiness, like being aware that they're urinating or having a bowel movement and telling about it, by staying "dry" for longer periods of time, and by showing *interest* in using the toilet. Also, we can assume that they may be "ready" when they start imitating other things their parents and older brothers and sisters do to care for themselves, things like washing themselves and brushing their own teeth.

It's sometimes hard for us parents not to measure a child's success by what the books say or by the standards of another sibling or a friend's child. The timetable for learning to use the potty for each child is as individual as learning to walk or talk. Expecting too much too soon can lead to frustration for both parents and children. If we make an effort to begin toilet training and find that our child isn't the least bit interested, it's probably a good idea to back off and try again later.

Accidents Are Natural

Even after children have learned to use the toilet, it's natural for them to have an "accident" once in a while. Even though toilet accidents are frustrating, children manage better when their parents are patient and remind them of their successes rather than making them feel bad when they've wet or soiled their pants. Children really do want to please their parents, and they like the feeling of "growing up."

It can take a long while for children to stay dry all through the night. That's usually because children sleep soundly, so they aren't aware of their bladder sensations. Many parents, before they go to sleep at night, find that it helps to wake a child to go to the bathroom.

One time I was visiting my son's nursery school class and the teacher said to the children: "Would anybody like to tell Mister Rogers something?" One little boy enthusiastically said, as if he had been waiting a long time to tell me, "Mister Rogers, I just wear diapers at night now." I think the teacher wondered what in the world I'd make of that little boy's offering. I said to him, "Thank you for telling me that. It's something very important, and of course it's up to you when you'll give up your diapers at night. I'm really proud of the ways you're growing." The little boy beamed, and there seemed to be a collective sigh from the rest of the children.

That way, children become used to the bladder sensations and learn to control themselves.

Even after they're "toilet trained," there may be times, like when they're sick or have a cold, that children will lapse into bedwetting. They have less control of their bladders when they aren't well or when they're upset about changes in their lives (like the arrival of a new baby in the family, a move from one home to another, or other stresses).

Training Is a Joint Effort

The "training" that goes on in "toilet training" is a joint effort. We parents train our children in the mechanics of using the toilet, but we also need to learn how to respond to their cues of being ready to be trained. Our children, on the other hand, have to develop an awareness of the sensations of urinating and having a bowel movement as well as developing a certain measure of muscular control.

When we parents are able to have realistic expectations, we are more likely to approach toilet training with a balance of gentleness and persistence, and our children are more likely to gain from the experience not only mastery of their body functions, but also a stronger sense of self. They can feel proud of themselves for the ways they are growing and learning to manage certain somethings that are important in the grownup world.

Helpful Hints

Starting Toilet Training:

■ Most children feel more comfortable using a potty chair that sits on the floor rather than a chair that sits on the toilet where they may worry they'll get flushed down the drain. Children also tend to feel better sitting on something that lets their feet touch the floor.

■ It can be very helpful to praise your child for getting to the bathroom on time. Many parents say things like, "I'm proud of you!" or "You really are growing!" Your praise means so much to your child. In fact, the main reasons children want to use the toilet are that they want to please the people they love and because they want to feel like they're growing up.

■ At first you may need to remind your child that it's time to stop playing and go to the bathroom. You might say something like, "I know it's hard to stop doing something you like, but it's really important to try to get to the bathroom on time."

■ You could help your child see his or her progress by putting stars or checkmarks on a calendar when he or she goes to the potty on time or stays dry all night.

Bedwetting:

■ Limit your child's liquids after dinner. Also, discourage your child from eating and drinking chocolate, sodas, or other foods with caffeine. Such things can make children urinate more often.

■ Have your child go to the bathroom just before going to sleep, and wake your child in the night to go again just before you yourself go to bed.

■ When you take your child to the bathroom in the middle of the night, let your child walk there. That may stimulate your child's awareness enough to find bladder control in the nighttime.

Dealing with Toilet Accidents:
■ Try to be patient with your child. It takes a while for many children to be completely toilet trained. At first accidents are common.

■ After an accident, give your child some of the clean-up work to do, like changing clothes or helping to wipe the area with a rag or paper towel. Being involved helps children know that it takes work and time to clean up from a toilet "accident."

■ Remember that accidents sometimes happen because of stressful changes in a child's life, like the arrival of a new baby brother or sister, changes in a parent's work hours, a move, a death in the family, or changes at a child care or preschool. The accidents will probably stop on their own, little by little, as children adjust to the changes.

■ Even though it's natural for parents to feel upset about accidents, it's important to try to be matter of fact about them. Many children already feel bad when they've had a toilet accident. It's important not to make them feel too ashamed to try the next time.

■ If you feel you need additional support, it can help to talk with a child care provider, pediatrician, or other parents. If you are concerned that the toilet accidents are going on too long, it's wise to check with your child's doctor or clinic.

The New Baby

"We were so excited to tell our three-year-old about the new baby who was to be born into the family. She caught us completely off guard when she asked, 'Who will be that baby's mommy?' I guess she was telling us she needed lots of reassurance that we'd still be her mother and father, and that we'd still love her even after the baby was born."

To a firstborn child, a family means three people—"mommy, daddy, me." When a new baby comes and starts to get a great deal of attention, it may still seem to the older child that the family is a threesome, but now it's "mommy, daddy, and that new baby." The "old baby" feels pushed out of the family triangle.

It's Hard to Share

Whether a baby is born or adopted into a family, there are many changes and many different feelings when the new child arrives. It's only natural that the children who are already there feel some resentment. They may even be angry with their parents and say things like, "Take the baby back!" or, "I hate you!" At any age, it's hard to share the people we love.

Parents sometimes tell me, "Oh, there's no jealousy. My child loves the baby." Well, love can be mixed with jealousy. Sometimes children are afraid that their parents might stop loving them if they show any "negative" feelings. What a relief it can be for a child to know that it's all right to be angry, sad, upset, or grumpy—all the while hearing that it's *not* all right to hurt the baby or anyone else. Our children (of all ages) need to hear that we love them even when they're experiencing difficult feelings.

Acting Like a Baby

Sometimes when there's a new baby in the family, the older child will seem to go backward in development—starting again to thumb-suck, bed-wet, cry a lot, or become extra-clinging. After all, those are the sorts of things babies do, and babies seem to get all the attention.

How much easier it would be if our children could say to us, "I'm really mad that you've brought home another baby. Wasn't I good enough for you? It feels like no one pays any attention to me any more!" But young children aren't able to use words to tell us how they're feeling. They can only feel it and then try to find some way to let those feelings out. Their anger and frustration may come out in ways that may not seem to have anything directly to do with the new baby. However, it's helpful to remember that when there are noticeable

A friend of mine told me about his three-year-old daughter Crystal's introduction to the new baby in her family. To help her play about being the "big sister," he and his wife gave her a new baby doll and were pleased that she brought it along to the hospital on her visit to see the baby for the first time.

The minute Crystal spotted the baby in her mother's arms, she began banging her baby doll against the wall. Her parents soon realized what she was telling them. Crystal's mother put the newborn in the crib and said, "You know what I need now? I need a hug." Dropping her doll, Crystal climbed up on the bed and snuggled into her mother's arms. It was deeply reassuring for her to know that even though the baby was now a very real part of the family, her parents still needed her love.

behavior changes in older children just after a baby's birth, we can be fairly sure that those changes have something to do with the new brother or sister's arrival.

Parents' Ambivalent Feelings

Some parents recognize their own ambivalence about having another child. They say that now and then, they feel they're betraying their firstborn or they wonder if they can handle raising another child. Just knowing those feelings are natural and normal can help us find healthy ways to manage them.

Most families discover that it can take several months for an older child to get used to the new baby. Hugs and loving words can go a long way in helping your older child through hard times. In the long run, with all the ups and downs of family life, brothers and sisters often develop an extra special relationship that enriches each of them throughout their lives.

Take Care of Yourself

There's so much to do in caring for all the usual needs of the family, and now there is a new baby! When you're exhausted and you don't feel your normal self physically (or hormonally), it's very hard to be kind and patient, and it can hurt your feelings when your older child gets angry at the new baby or at you. Your own rest is one of the most important things to help you cope, so when your older child is sleeping, do all you can to get some rest yourself. Hopefully, you're able to ask for help from relatives and friends when you feel you need it. It takes a lot of inner strength to say that you need help. People who love you are delighted when you can, and do.

Helpful Hints

Before the Baby Arrives:

■ It's probably a good idea to wait as long as you can to tell your child about a new baby coming. Young children don't understand time the way adults do, and it's hard for them to wait for events long in the future.

■ Let your child know what to expect from newborns: they sleep a lot, they cry, they can't play games or talk, and grownups have to do almost everything for them. If you know of another family with a new baby, you might want to make a short visit so your child can see firsthand what an infant can and cannot do. "Sibling classes," available at hospitals for big brothers and sisters, can be helpful, too.

Arriving Home:

■ Let someone else carry the baby into the house so you can give your full attention to your older child. Some parents are surprised when they get a "cold shoulder" or an angry "hello." That's usually a child's way of saying, "I love you so much. I'm mad at you for leaving me and for loving another baby."

■ Spend time with your older child. Set aside "just you and me" times, like when the baby is sleeping. When children know they can count on one-on-one time somewhere during the day, they may be able to manage better through the other times. Moments when you're listening carefully—even times when you're doing something simple like zipping up your child's jacket—can say, "I still love you, no matter what."

■ Let your child hear, "You have a special place in our family, and the baby does, too." That helps children know that no one will ever take their place. In fact, your firstborn child might feel especially proud to know he or she was the one who made you a "parent" in the first place.

■ Let your child know it's okay to be angry or upset and grumpy about the new baby, but it's never okay to hurt the baby. It's very scary for children to think they might hurt the baby. In general, young children can't be trusted with the new baby without an adult's supervision. It is absolutely essential for them to know that you will not let them hurt the baby, just as you will not let anyone ever hurt them.

■ Encourage your child to find healthy ways to express feelings about the baby. An appropriate, wonderful gift for an older child is a realistic-looking infant baby doll. Whether your child is a boy or girl, the doll can encourage some helpful play about being a caring mother or father. Don't be surprised if there's some spanking or rough play with the doll. You might also see a lot of different feelings coming out in drawings, puppet play, or make-believe play. These are healthy ways to say how they feel—ways that don't hurt the baby or anyone else.

■ Help your child feel proud of being the older one. Show your appreciation for all the things he or she *can* do that the baby *can't* yet do, like going for a walk, sharing treats, playing with toys, and using words to say what he or she is thinking, doing, and feeling.

■ Involve your child in caring for the baby. Encourage your child to sing or talk to the baby, get the diapers, and play peek-a-boo. Point out times when the baby stopped crying or laughed because of something your older child did. When children are given ways to help with the baby, they feel more grownup, needed, and special.

Adjusting to Child Care

*"At first when I dropped my son off at child care, he said 'goodbye' and practically pushed me out the door. But when the next Monday came, he did a complete turn-around—crying and clinging. His caregiver told me that some children hold in their fears and feelings at first, and being home on the weekend can remind them how much they like being with the family. She suggested that instead of telling him that **he** seemed to need me to stay a while, it could be helpful to say that **I** needed to spend some more time there in the mornings. For the next couple of weeks, I stayed a bit longer, and my son seemed to feel much better when it was time for me to say goodbye. Frankly, I did, too."*

Children feel safe when they are with family or others they know well. So many children have a hard time if and when they start child care. Child care is a new place with new people. It's not until the age of three that children begin to get a confident sense of their own separateness from everyone else. It's not surprising then that during the first three years, separation from parents (the people whom a child feels closest to and even feels part of) can be very upsetting for a child.

Trust Takes Time

It naturally takes time before children can feel secure in a child-care setting. They can't feel safe until they trust their new caregivers, and they can't trust them until they come to know them and feel "related" to them. Trust builds over time. For some children, building trust takes longer than for others.

Since children don't understand the child care routine at first, they don't know when parents will come back, or *if* parents will come back. When children learn, day by day, that their parents come for them when they say they will, they also learn to trust that times of separation will be followed by times of being together again.

Children grow in their ability to handle transitions when we let them know that it's okay to feel sad and angry at first, and that little by little, they'll feel better and find different things to enjoy. If grownups make children feel babyish for crying or being sad, those children may get even more upset. When children hear that their feelings are natural and normal, they are more likely to manage better.

Create Transition Routines

Some families use rituals and routines to help smooth transitions. Some have special ways of saying goodbye with certain "secret" family words, gestures, or hugs. Many parents create a routine of taking their children into the child care setting themselves, helping them take off their coats, getting them settled, and giving them a hug and a reminder that they'll be back later in the day. When "goodbye" gets to

A mother told us that she was surprised by her daughter's reaction when she came to pick her up the first few days of child care. She expected a joyful reunion, especially since her child had such trouble saying goodbye in the morning. Instead, her three-year-old hid under a table and came out only after a lot of coaxing. Her caregiver explained that some children seem to need to say, "I'm still upset that you left me. Now I'm the one who is not leaving." She assured the mom that her daughter was glad to see her, even if it didn't always look like it. As her daughter grew more confident at child care, her "goodbyes" and "hellos" grew warmer. Soon she was running to her mother at the end of the day, hugging her legs and chattering away about something she made.

mean "I'll be back later," it becomes a much better word.

Think about what has helped your child handle other comings and goings in the past. Even though each situation is different, the transition into child care or preschool is much like other separations your child has already experienced, like going to bed at night, having a babysitter, or playing at a friend's home. This new separation is also much like those that will happen in the future—going off to college and leaving home much later in life. The caring way you help your child adjust to child care or preschool is strengthening the foundation for the transitions your child will be dealing with in all the years to come.

Letting Go Is Hard for Parents, Too

For many parents, child care is a necessity, but even those who put their very young children in someone else's care by choice have many mixed feelings. Most parents feel some guilt or are upset by the thought that they're missing out on the joy of helping their children learn new things and watching them make the everyday discoveries that are so delightful in childhood.

There can be many reasons why it's hard for parents to let go. Sometimes it's even difficult to know who's having the greater problem saying goodbye, the child or the parent. If you talk about your concerns with your child's caregiver, you may find that many other parents have those same feelings. Knowing that our feelings are natural and normal helps all of us feel more confident, which in turn helps our children manage better, too.

Developing a Partnership

Watching a close bond forming between a child and a new caregiver can bring pangs of jealousy to any parent. But the love between a parent and child is unique. No matter how attached a young child may become to another caregiver, it will be a different kind of attachment than the one the child feels to his or her mother or father. No one else can ever take your place.

If you've chosen high quality child care, you're giving your child the opportunity to learn that there are other adults besides their parents who are loving and can be trusted. One thing's for sure—for day care to be a healthy part of a child's growth, parents and child care providers need to work together closely. They must be partners in helping children as they grow.

Helpful Hints

Before the First Day of Child Care:

■ Visit the child-care center with your child before his or her care starts, and stay there for a while with your child. Your child can feel more secure with you nearby, and therefore more willing to get to know the people there.

■ Let your child see that you're friendly with the caregiver. If you can spend time talking and smiling with each other, then your child sees that you like and trust each other.

■ Show your child all the rooms that the class uses—especially the bathroom and the kitchen. Let your child see that in many ways, the child-care setting is similar to home. Children feel more comfortable when they see that there are familiar home-like things in a new place.

When Child Care Starts:

■ Plan to stay with your child a while for the first few days or more. It may help if you gradually stay a bit less each day. Of course, some children need a longer time before they feel comfortable in a new place.

■ Some children like to bring along a stuffed animal, favorite toy, or their beloved "blankey." It's comforting to have something that's a part of home there, even if that toy has to stay in a "cubby."

■ While it may seem easier at first just to slip out the door with no goodbye, that may make separation more difficult. Your child will likely have a harder time trusting when you will go and when you will come back.

■ Remember that there are certain times that your child may need extra help with adjusting—after a weekend at home, holiday vacations, an illness, when there's a substitute teacher, or when the group moves on to another room, even if it's in the same center.

■ At the end of the day, some children need a little more time to stop playing. It helps if you can stay a little and show an interest in what your child is doing.

Going to the Doctor

"The last couple of times that my daughter had a doctor's appointment, she cried and carried on. I kept asking what she didn't like about going to the doctor, and she finally told me she was scared of getting a shot. So next time when she has a checkup scheduled, I'm going to call the doctor's office beforehand to see if she needs a shot. If not, I can assure her that it's not going to happen this time. If she does need a shot, I can prepare her for it a day or so before and maybe let her use her doctor's kit to play about giving an injection to me or to her dolls."

Even though your child may have been going to the doctor since birth, and even though you have a caring doctor, there may come a time when a check-up becomes particularly upsetting. As children grow physically, they also grow in awareness of their own bodies and their ability to remember painful past experiences. At the same time, in those pre-school years, they have many fantasies and misconceptions.

Children's Fantasies

Some parents have wondered why their children get upset when a medical professional looks into their ears with an otoscope, listens to their hearts with a stethoscope, or takes X-ray pictures. Most likely it's because children often worry that doctors can see or hear what they're thinking and feeling when they look inside them or listen to their hearts or read their X-rays. It's important for children to know that no equipment can tell what they're thinking or feeling. People's thoughts and feelings are their own—to share or not to share—with whomever they wish.

A common childhood fantasy is that whatever is under the skin could all leak out if the skin gets punctured or cut. Some children worry that their whole "insides" will come out even if they get a tiny cut. We need to let children know that this can't happen. We also need to tell them that the doctor or nurse takes only a little bit of blood during bloodtests. Children need help in understanding that after a needle prick, there's still as much blood as a person needs left on the inside, and our skin heals and closes and won't let any more come out. Also, a child can be reassured by having little bandage, which seems to keep everything inside where it's supposed to be.

Caring Preparation

Children don't like to be probed and poked, especially when the probing and the poking happen unexpectedly. And they certainly don't like to have painful or uncomfortable things happening to them. Injections ("shots") hurt, if just for a moment, stethoscopes are often cold on a chest, and blood pressure cuffs often squeeze an arm. Everyone is better able to manage if we're prepared by knowing what may hurt as well as what probably won't hurt.

When children discover that we've been honest with them in preparing them for experiences, they grow in their trust not only of us, but also of their doctors, nurses, and other medical professionals. That trust will help them all through their life, as they begin to assume responsibility for their own health care needs.

*F*or the **Neighborhood** programs, we made a video segment to help explain an emergency room to children in case they should ever have to visit one. Before we turned on the cameras, there was a young boy in the emergency department where we were videotaping, and he started telling me what had happened to a friend of his. He explained that he and his friend were both smart, but that his friend had fallen down and cut his head so that nearly all of his brains had come out. He told me his friend wouldn't be smart any more if all of his brains came out. Children's fantasies about what might happen to them are often much scarier than the reality!

Parents' Concerns

Parents might have some anxiety, too, when they take their child to the doctor. One of the most basic responsibilities of parenting is to see that our children are healthy. So when the doctor tells us that our child is "developing on track and thriving," that's a reassurance that we're "good parents." But there's also a chance that the doctor might find something to be concerned about. Along with the worries about a child's physical health, the words: "Something's wrong" are too easily translated as, "Something's wrong with my parenting."

It's important to have a trusting relationship with the people on your child's medical team. You need to feel comfortable with the way your questions and concerns are answered, and to trust that you're providing your child with the best medical care you can.

Making Shots More Manageable

Parents often tell me that they dread their child's doctor appointment because their child may need an immunization. They may even feel guilty for cooperating with the doctor in inflicting that "pain" on their child. A lot of parents are afraid that their child will get upset if they talk about the examination, and particularly the "shot," beforehand. But there are ways to talk about such things, and there are ways to help children manage them. You might ask your child to try to think of ideas that might help make the "pinch" easier to take. Maybe by sitting in your lap, holding on to a "blankey" from home, singing a song really loudly, or taking along a stuffed animal or baby doll to get a pretend shot first! It may also help if you remind your child that the pinch of the injection hurts for only a moment, and then the hurt goes away. You could also explain that an injection puts medicine into our bodies and that certain medicines work better when they're given that way. We take some medicine in our mouths, some with patches, and others with injections. Doctors and nurses know which kinds to give us to keep us healthy. Children don't need elaborate explanations—they're generally satisfied with simple, honest answers. It can be a good feeling to give your child some "tools" that make a difference in how he or she handles a difficult experience!

Of course, we can't anticipate all that will happen in a doctor's office, but we can be honest about what we do know. Our children trust us more and more each time they find that we're doing our best to prepare them for whatever they have to go through.

Helpful Hints

Before Going to the Doctor:

■ Talk about doctors and nurses kindly so your child hears that health professionals are "on your team." Children also like to know that doctors and nurses were children once, too. They know what it's like to be a child, and they studied a long time to learn how to help people be healthy. Children might also feel reassured to hear that some doctors and nurses are mothers and fathers with children of their own that they care for and love.

■ A day or so before going to the doctor, mention the upcoming visit. Talk about what your child can expect, like the doctor's equipment, possible procedures, and even the waiting room. Let your child know that you will be right there the whole time.

■ Encourage your child to play about being the doctor for stuffed animals or for other family members. In their play, children are in control, and when they are, they don't feel so helpless. As they play, they often "rehearse" the procedures, which helps them work on their feelings.

At the Doctor's Office:

■ If there aren't toys in the waiting room, bring along a few small playthings, a notebook and pencil, and maybe some snack foods.

■ Suggest that your child bring along a "blankey" or stuffed animal. Those things can be comforting.

■ Some children have a hard time taking off their clothes because it makes them feel too vulnerable. They may also have a growing need for body privacy.

After the Doctor's Office:

■ When the doctor visit is over and you're on your way home, encourage your child to talk about what happened. Once you're home, your child may want to tell others in the family as well. Freely talking about the appointment can be very helpful. In fact, whatever difficult things children talk about can be made much more manageable just by talking and listening.

■ Doctor or dentist play after appointments is just as important as playing beforehand. Adults most often handle stressful experiences by talking about them, but young children also play about them and draw pictures about them. They might even want to give comfort to their dolls or stuffed animals, very much like you've comforted them.

Going to the Dentist

"During his first dental appointment, our three-year-old son was so anxious that he wouldn't even say hello to the dentist. But after the dentist mentioned something about the water being cold while she was washing her hands, our son started chatting away with her. It was as if he had just realized that the dentist wasn't a scary creature—that she had real feelings, just like her patients!"

One of the first ways we human beings learn about the world is through our mouths. In fact, our earliest pleasure comes through our mouths. The experience of that early feeding influences us forever. All through life we use our mouths for eating, for talking, for expressing feelings, and for showing affection.

"I Like to Be Told"

It's not surprising that children have concerns about a visit to the dentist. It's a place where someone not only looks in their mouths but puts fingers and tools in there, too. Just as with any other new experience, it's helpful to prepare children for what to expect. They'll trust us more and more as they find that the things we tell them are true.

It helps children to hear ahead of time about some of the unfamiliar things they'll see in the dentist's office—the bright light, the

chair that goes up and down, the tray of sharp-looking instruments, the little hoses that squirt either air or water or act like a vacuum cleaner for their mouth. Often it's the small things that we adults take for granted that may be the biggest concern for a child. A bib that suddenly gets clipped around the neck, for instance, might make a child wonder if he or she is going to be turned into a baby again. The bright intense light shining in their eyes may also upset them.

Usually during the first visit the dentist will need only to take a good look at your child's mouth, count your child's teeth, and possibly do a simple cleaning procedure. At that time, potential problems can be spotted so they can be corrected later. Because dentists generally don't do "treatments" on a first visit, that's a good time for children to get used to sitting in the dentist's chair and seeing what it's like to have someone look into their mouths.

Controlling the Urge to Bite

Many young children are likely to be wrestling with their natural urge to bite, and a dental exam may test their self-control. Biting is a way that some young children have of saying, "I'm angry," and it may be their only way to express their anger until they're able to use words well. Even children who have learned to control their urge to bite may feel angry when

Dear Tooth Fairy,
Here is my tooth. It fell out in school today. It was a front one right in the middle. It was loose for a long time. I kept wiggling it. The teacher put it in an envelope. Here it is.
Love, Becca

Becca's mom told me about her family's tradition of leaving notes for the "tooth fairy." She said, "When our children were little, we always made a big deal of the 'tooth fairy'—after all, that tooth was once part of them. The 'tooth fairy' always sent them a thank-you note. I think they liked the notes as much as the coins that came along with them!" With or without the "tooth fairy," there are lots of ways to give a lost tooth a kind of importance, even when it's gone— like marking the date on a "growing chart" or using a special plate or cup at dinner when a child has something to celebrate.

someone makes them open their mouths when they don't want to. They know they shouldn't bite, but they're not sure that they can control that feeling. It can be scary for them to think they might hurt someone whose fingers are in their mouth.

Taking Care of Yourself

During their lifetime, children will meet many health care professionals like dentists and dental hygienists. Little by little children can learn that they are worth taking care of. That's what makes them want to eat healthy foods, brush and floss regularly, and have checkups. When they feel that they are people who are worth taking care of, they are much more likely to grow into adults who will take good care of themselves.

Trust Between Parents and Dentists

It may be hard for some of us parents to help our children have positive attitudes about the dentist when we ourselves are dealing with our own memories and concerns about drilling, needles, or pain. Of course, dentistry today is different than when some of us were children.

Today, most routine dental work that a child needs is practically painless.

Your reassurance can be especially helpful for your child. Of course, if you're calm and confident about the dentist or hygienist and if you can be right there with your child, you're offering the best emotional support of all.

As children begin to manage dental procedures, the biggest help will be a trusting relationship with the dentist and the dental hygienist. That's why it's important to choose a dentist who cares about children and their special needs. If you as a parent feel good about a dentist, the chances are your child will sense your confidence and have positive feelings, too.

Helpful Hints

■ Help your child know what to expect. Talk about the fancy chair and some of the dental tools, like the little mirror on a handle, the special electric toothbrush, and the water squirter for rinsing teeth. You may want to ask a librarian for books about the dentist's office so your child can see what some of the equipment looks like. You may also want to let your child know that each dentist's office is different and won't look exactly like the one in the books.

■ Let your child know about the waiting room, too. It would be a good idea to take along one or two small toys or a notebook in case there are no playthings and you have to wait a while to begin the appointment.

■ Encourage your child to play about being the dentist with a doll or stuffed animal. When children play about being the dentist, they are in charge of what happens and they might not feel so helpless when they are the patients.

■ Before your child's first dental appointment, you may want to consider taking your child along with you when you have a dental cleaning so your child can know what to expect.

■ If you think your child may be especially upset during a visit to the dentist, it's good to call the dentist or hygienist and talk about it beforehand. They like to be told if you or your child have special concerns.

Caring for Teeth at Home

■ Brushing teeth properly is a key to having healthy teeth, and children need help with that. Encourage your child to start brushing his or her teeth, even though you may have to finish the job. You'll need to help with flossing, too. Children often find it fun to brush and floss because they are "grownup" things to do.

■ Encourage your child to eat and drink foods like milk and crunchy fruits and vegetables that help to grow strong and healthy teeth. These foods make the best between-meal snacks, too.

■ Talk with your child about the difference between foods that are always good for us, like fruits and vegetables, and foods like candy and sweets that should be eaten only as an occasional treat.

■ Encourage your child to brush and rinse after meals and particularly after eating sweet or sticky foods.

Starting Kindergarten

"One of the neighbor kids told our daughter that she had to know all her ABCs before she started school. That really scared her. I wanted her to have a more positive image, so after talking with her about her fears, we started playing 'school' at home, and I let her be the teacher. It was fascinating to see what kind of teacher she pretended to be. That helped me talk with her about some of the teachers I had when I was a child and some of the things I enjoyed doing at school."

Most children are eager to learn and to join the world of the bigger kids who already go to school. But, like other big steps in life, beginning school can arouse many different feelings. Some children even imagine that being sent to school is a kind of punishment. They may wonder if they are somehow less important now because they're being "sent away," and they may feel jealous of younger brothers or sisters who get to spend the whole day playing at home.

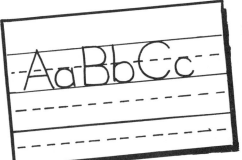

Children's Misconceptions about School

Some children are afraid to go to school because they don't know how to read and work with numbers, and they think they have to know all those things before they even arrive at school. Other children worry that there won't be any time for play once they get to school, or that they won't know when it's time to go home. They may worry about what could happen if they don't listen to the teacher, or what they should do if they have to go to the bathroom. It's helpful to encourage our children to talk about their concerns or fears so we can answer their questions, correct their misconceptions, and give them more realistic expectations.

We can let them know that going to school is like discovering a new world, but not a world that's completely unfamiliar. The more we help them recognize how much school is like home, the easier the transition can be. Like home, school has places to sit, places to play, a kitchen, bathrooms, and grownups (teachers) who care about children.

A Step Forward, a Step Back

When children feel uncertain about a new experience like kindergarten, it's common for them to behave in ways that they did when they were much younger—clinging to their caregivers more closely than usual, thumb-sucking again, or even forgetting toilet training now and then. It helps to remember that such steps backward often come before big strides forward in a child's development.

Letting Go Can Be Hard for Parents

Parents, too, confront major milestones when their children enter kindergarten. It can be hard to face the fact that "my baby" is growing up. Many parents find it very difficult to "let go" those first days of school. They may even be remembering their own first days of separation from their own parents! No wonder there are many teary-eyed mothers and fathers each year when school begins!

No matter how well things are going for your child at school, it can be very helpful to take the time to get to know your child's teacher

A five-year-old boy named Eric asked me, "Is school nice? Is school fun?" I said that all schools are different, but that teachers are people who care about children and try to make things happen in ways that are best for the children in their classrooms. I also told him that some things at school can be fun and exciting, but there's another kind of fun that is quiet and can give children a good feeling about thinking, working, and learning. In fact, one of the best feelings in the world is being proud of what you've learned after you've worked hard to learn it. If we can help children think of hard work as a different kind of "fun," they're more likely to find the energies to keep on working and trying, and discovering the joy in accomplishing something that took great effort.

and principal. Your child can sense when you're all working together "on the same team." If you have a good relationship with the teacher, you will probably feel more comfortable talking with him or her about your child's progress or special concerns.

Asking and Listening

As children deal with the different challenges of school, it can help them to know that we adults will gladly listen to what their day was like. Children need to know that their parents care about what happens at school and that their family is proud of the ways they're learning.

There may be days, of course, when children won't want to talk at all about school, but if you've listened before, your child can trust that you will want to again when he or she is ready.

Share Your Own Experiences

Helping a child get ready for school often brings back feelings we adults had when we began school. No matter what those feelings are, if we can accept them truthfully and share them with our children, we can each have another important opportunity to grow. "I felt that way, too, when I was a child. Tell me more about what your day was like," is a wonderful way to begin to work on any new kind of growing.

Helpful Hints

Before the First Day of School:

■ Try to find a balance between acknowledging your child's fears and talking about school and teachers in warm and positive ways. You might ask what your child thinks school will be like so you can try to clear up any misconceptions.

■ If you possibly can, call the school and set up a visit so that you and your child can meet the teacher and tour the school building to see the classroom and other places (like the gym, the playground, the kitchen, and the bathroom). It can be reassuring for children to know that many teachers are parents (and grandparents) themselves, that they were children once, too, and that it took a lot of learning for them to become teachers.

■ Help your child get to know other children in the neighborhood who go to the same school. You might try to arrange a "play date" with another child who will be in the same class, so your child will know at least one other classmate that first day.

■ Prepare your child for some of the rules at school. Let your child know that teachers often make rules to help children be safe or to make learning orderly. One common rule is that children have to raise their hand and wait to be called on before they speak so that the teacher can be sure that everyone gets a turn.

■ Help your child learn your family's address and phone number. Write them on a paper and tape it inside your child's pencil case or backpack. It's reassuring for children to know that they have that information.

■ Walk or ride with your child to school and back, so your child can become familiar with the route. You might also want to introduce your child to the crossing guard or school bus driver. Children often find that crossing guards and bus drivers become trusted friends.

Just Before School Begins:

■ To help the morning go smoothly, get things ready the night before—pack lunch, pick out clothes, set the breakfast table.

■ Send your child off with encouraging words like "Have a good day" rather than warnings like "You better be good."

■ If you pack a lunch, you might want to include a kind note or a small toy. Things from home can be a comfort when your child feels homesick. Some parents paste a photograph of the whole family in their child's lunchbox as a reminder that the family will be together again at the end of the day.

After School:

■ Encourage your child to talk about the day's activities, and really listen to what he or she says. Ask things like, "What was fun, what was not fun?" or "What was easy, what was hard?" Keep in mind that children often love to exaggerate about how "bad" the other children were or how "mean" the teacher was. Try to remember what it was like for you.

■ If you hear that something was difficult at school, let your child know that you understand there are some things at school that are hard to do, that you're proud that he or she has been trying, and that tomorrow will be a new and hopefully better day.

Special Challenges

Some things in life are especially hard to deal with, and especially hard to talk about, for adults as well as for children. It seems that the most difficult things have to do with loss. While most often "going away" is followed by "coming back," there are times when it's not, like the death of a loved one, or a divorce, or a move to a new home. When a loss is permanent, children can feel a lot of anger and sadness about whatever or whomever has been taken away.

When we can help children talk about their "worries" and their feelings, we help them know that they are not alone, that their thoughts are normal, and that there are many healthy ways to deal with what they might be thinking and feeling. Whatever is mentionable can be much more manageable. And what a big relief it is for children when they learn to talk and play about their feelings! If they're able to do that when they're young, they take that "gift" with them all through life. When strong winds blow, that inner gift can often make the difference between bending and breaking.

Moving

"Boy, were we surprised by how our children reacted to the move! We were most worried about how the move would affect our second-grader because she had to leave the friends and teachers she liked so much at school. As it turned out, our second-grader adjusted rather well. It was the toddler who seemed the most upset!"

Some adults and children like the adventure of a new home right from the start. Others take longer to adjust. Moving can be especially hard for young children. They consider their home and the things around them as part of them. For young children, "my" is "me," so they feel very much attached to their bed, the window in the bedroom, even the stairs. When families move, children often feel like part of themselves is left behind.

Lots of Feelings about Moving

Some parents are reluctant to bring up anything negative about a move, thinking that if they don't mention how sad it is to leave, the children won't feel sad. But it's natural for everyone to have some sad feelings about a move. If we talk only about the exciting things and not at all about the sad ones, children may think there's something wrong with them for feeling sad. But if we let them know that it's very natural to feel sad and happy about the same thing (like moving) they're likely to be able to find some of the happy things about the move.

One time when our family had to move, I told our sons that so many people have felt two ways about the same thing (happy *and* sad) that there was even a word for it in our language. The word is "ambivalent." The boys latched onto that word and made it theirs! "I really feel ambivalent about this move," they'd often say—like a code—which, of course, meant, "I don't feel all good about it, but I don't feel all bad about it either."

Children can also be angry about all the changes. In fact, anger is a natural reaction to loss. It's important that we do what we can to help them find constructive ways to deal with their anger by encouraging them to use words, pound play clay, or make up a song or a dance. As with other angry times, we can let them know that it's okay to be angry, but it's not okay to hurt themselves or others. Such limits can be comforting to children. If you don't allow them to hurt anyone else, they'll come to understand that you won't let anyone else hurt them, either.

Linda is a former colleague of mine. Years ago she shared with me this story of their toddler's behavior when they moved.

Linda, her husband, and Whitney arrived at their new home before the moving van arrived. When they went inside, Whitney clung to his mother and father, insisting on keeping both of them in sight at all times. Even with their constant attention, he cried a great deal and was generally miserable— and so were they.

But when the moving van finally arrived at the new home, Whitney's behavior changed dramatically. The furniture from their former home was carried into the new house, and Whitney greeted their old sofa with a crow of delight. From the sound of his babbling, he was obviously having a reunion with an old and important friend: "How are you? You don't know how I've missed you! I'm so glad you're here!" Whitney had a lot more feelings about the move to work out, but from the time the sofa got into the living room he was much more comfortable, and he began taking his first emotional steps toward accepting his new home.

Understanding Temporary Setbacks

When children feel the normal stress of moving, one of the most common ways they react is by regressing—becoming more dependent, clingy, and whiny, sucking their thumbs and crying. They often lose abilities they've just acquired, like toilet training or sleeping through the night. Regression is their way of showing that they want to go back to a safer and more comfortable time. Usually the regression is a temporary setback until the new place feels like home.

Stressful for Parents, Too

On any list of "stresses" in adult life, you'll find moving very near the top. There's so much to do! And so much to feel! Even if there are some exciting things about going to a new home, there's almost always some ambivalence.

Even though parents may have some sad and angry feelings, if they feel somewhat optimistic about a move, chances are that their children will share in their enthusiasm. Of course, we shouldn't hide our true feelings from our children by pretending to feel something we don't feel. One of the most important, helpful things we can do if we're angry or sad is to let our children know that *they* are not the cause of our anger or sadness. They need to know that they are loved, and that together the whole family can try to make the best of the move. Knowing that they "belong" and that their parents are counting on them during any time of transition can be an enormous boost to their growing sense of self. Over time, everyone in the family will come to terms with the move in his or her own way, at his or her own pace.

Helpful Hints

Before the Move:

■ Children may have misconceptions about what goes to the new home and what doesn't. Some children think that important things like the bathtub and sink go to the new home! When you talk about the things that will go and the things that will stay, you might want to tell your child about the fixtures (like a bathtub and a sink) that will be waiting for them in the new place. Also, reassure them that the things you do take along will be carefully packed in boxes for the trip.

■ If you can, visit the new home with your child. If you can't, try to show your child some photographs. Talk about where the furniture will fit in the new rooms.

■ Help your child pack a separate box or bag of special toys or clothes to take with you in the car or plane. Then your child can be really sure those things will not be left behind.

■ Talk about what to expect on moving day. Encourage your child to play about moving. An empty box or toy truck can be a pretend moving truck. When children play, they're in charge of what happens. Playing also gives them a chance to rehearse some of their feelings about the move. This kind of activity can be as helpful after the move, too. While adults use words to talk about what's stressful, children are much more likely to express their feelings through their play.

In the New Home:
■ Where possible, let your child decide some things for his or her bedroom, like what color to paint the room or where to put the bed or bookshelves. Even small decisions, like where to put certain toys or a poster, can be important to a child. It can help children feel more secure if you set up their room first.

■ Give your child easy things to unpack and put away. Children like to know that they are helpful.

■ In the midst of all the hectic work of moving, it can be hard to find fun things to do with your child. Here are some easy ideas:
Have a picnic on a blanket in
  an empty room.
Pack a meal in a lunch box.
Make a cozy corner with a blanket
  or sleeping bag for rest time.

■ Help your child stay in touch with old friends by sending drawings, writing letters, e-mailing, or making phone calls. From time to time, your child might appreciate looking back at photos of people, places, and things from the old neighborhood. You might want to make a special photo album or scrapbook for your child.

■ Let your child know that neighbors may come around to see who's moving in. The arrival of a moving truck in a neighborhood usually attracts families with children. Everyone wants to see who the new neighbors are— "maybe there's a friend for me!" You might want to have a box of cookies or pretzels on hand to offer to visitors. Hospitality goes a long way towards making friends.

■ Visit places in your community where families gather, like the library or a play-ground, to help your child find playmates. New friends can make a new place feel more like "home."

Adoption

"Our adopted child is one year old now, and we're trying to figure out the best time to let him know he was adopted, and how we can talk about it with him. I started telling him a story about a little boy who was adopted so he can get used to hearing the word 'adopted.' It's also helped me get used to saying it to him."

Being adopted into a caring family can be a very special "love story." But adoption can be difficult to talk about, since it involves one of a child's deepest needs: the sense of security in belonging to a family that will always take care of him or her.

Talking about Adoption

Each child has unique ways of dealing with being adopted, and those ways can change as children grow. Some children talk a lot about being adopted, and they ask a lot of questions. Other children are quite quiet about it.

Some people tell "the story of when you were adopted" as they're rocking their infants or when they're snuggling with their toddler. Of course, infants and toddlers don't understand much about what's being said; nevertheless they're hearing about their history in a natural way.

Some parents worry that if they don't talk about adoption with their adopted child early on, someone else may reveal it to their child and that could raise even more concerns for him or her. In fact, a child could feel betrayed and wonder if adoption might be something shameful or something to hide if he or she hears such an important thing from someone other than family.

"It's not your fault . . ."

As children grow, they try to make their own sense of why they were adopted. During the preschool years, as they work on controlling their own "bad" behavior, adopted children sometimes wonder if their birthparents didn't keep them because they were "bad" or because they cried a lot. Those children need a lot of assurance from adults that what they're thinking just isn't true. It's better to say, "Your birthmother and birthfather just weren't able to take care of any baby at all," rather than saying, "Your birthmother and birthfather couldn't take care of *you*." In other words, there was nothing wrong with your child in particular; rather, it was the birthparents' inability to provide care that prompted the adoption. If children are left to their own fantasies and think they were abandoned because they were bad, their next unspoken question to their adoptive parents might be, "How bad do I have to be before *you* give me away, too?"

Children need to hear that there were probably many reasons why their birth parents couldn't take care of a child, but that those reasons all have to do with the grownups. You may want to ask your child why he or she thinks some birthparents can't care for a baby, so you can correct any misconceptions and maybe find out more about what your child really wants to know.

Adoption Is for Always

There are wonderful things about being adopted into a loving family; nevertheless, some children feel that adoption also means loss—loss of relationships with people they didn't even know, people who were a significant part of

A father told me that he cringes when people who hear that their son is adopted say, "He is so lucky to have you as a parent." He explained, "They make me feel as if I'm some kind of extraordinarily wonderful parent, and I'm not. I'm just a regular parent. Just like all other parents, my wife and I have ups and downs, times when we make mistakes, and times when we handle things well. We're human beings, just like every other parent in this world."

their history. Some children have said to their adoptive mother, "I'm sad that I didn't grow in your tummy." Adoptive mothers can let them know that they're sad about that, too, (if in fact they are) but that they're also very glad that "you're growing in our family!"

Many families nowadays avoid saying "You were chosen" because that could imply that those adopted children are expected to live up to certain expectations if they are to remain chosen. Parents may think they're helping their child feel secure by believing they are "chosen," but oddly enough, that can have just the opposite effect. Adopted children need to hear and to know that adoption is not conditional—adoption is for always. They need to hear, "You are special, not because you're adopted, but just because you're you. No matter what, you will always be part of our family. Adoption is for keeps."

Parents' Feelings about Adoption

For most adoptive parents, the process of adoption involves working on the resolution of some of their own feelings—feelings of "failure" at not having borne a child, or recognizing that their child has a history that they may not know outside of the adopted family. While some people deal with many of those feelings as they go through the adoption process, it might surprise them to find some of the same things surfacing again and again.

One of the most difficult things for adoptive parents to hear from their adopted child is, "You're not my real mother. I don't have to listen to you!" When children say such things, they may be reacting out of their hurt, their longing, or their fear of their unknown past. The interesting thing is that their child's reaction is a natural reaction for *any* child when a parent says "no" to something he or she wants! Almost all children, whether they were adopted or not, fantasize that their "real" parents were kind, loving, perfect people who surely would have let them do anything they want. Children need to hear, "I'm not your birthparent, but I am your real parent who loves you and takes care of you!" Though our children may protest our limits and rules, they will feel much more secure when they know their parents are standing firm.

As the years go on and their children develop in many ways, parents often say that it helps to know some general things about child development so they don't have to attribute every "challenge" in the family to the adoption.

Helpful Hints

Talking about Adoption

■ Find natural opportunities to talk about adoption, like when you're rocking the baby, looking at photos, or going through momentos. Let your child know that you wanted a child very much and that you did a lot of preparation to get ready for a child to come into your family.

■ Adopted children need to know that they were born, just like every other baby in the world. It's reassuring for them to know they had the same beginnings as everyone else.

■ When you're talking about your child's beginnings, it's helpful for children to understand that it takes a man and a woman to make a baby.

■ It's all right to say, "I don't know," if your child asks, "What were my birthparents like?" or "When I grow up, will I have babies grow inside of me or adopt?" or "Did my birth parents have other babies?" There's a lot we don't know, a lot we may *never* know, and while that may be frustrating for children, they learn that it's possible to live with unanswered questions. The important thing is that they know we care about them, their questions, and their feelings.

■ If your child is from another culture, another country, or another race, it can help to find out about that culture's food, songs, holidays, and rituals so you can help your child feel connected to and proud of his or her original heritage. Many parents who have adopted internationally enjoy sharing experiences with other similar families through support groups or friendships.

■ Some adopted children think that everyone else in the world is adopted, too. Most young children assume that the rest of the world is just like them and their family.

Celebrate your Child's Adoption

■ Make a photo album for your child. Most children love to look at pictures of themselves as a baby and as they were growing, and they often delight in hearing the story of "the day we adopted you."

■ Many families commemorate the anniversary date of the adoption in addition to the child's birthday. They sometimes have a special meal. Afterwards they tell the story of how their child came into the family. That is a day to celebrate!

Tragic Events in the News

*"On September 11th, I had the television on much of the morning. My four-year-old was playing near me, but I didn't think she knew what was happening. I told her it was a plane crash. Every now and then she'd look up at the TV. Then she said **a lot** of planes were crashing. She didn't know that the same video was being repeated over and over again! I realized that for her sake, I'd better turn off the television; when I wanted to hear what was going on, I'd just turn on the radio for a few minutes. Actually, I felt better with the television off, too."*

In times of

community or worldwide crisis, it's easy to assume that young children don't know what's going on. But one thing's for sure—children are very sensitive to how their parents feel. They're keenly aware of the expressions on their parents' faces and the tone of their voices. Children sense when their parents are really worried, whether they're watching the news or talking about it with others. No matter what children know about a "crisis," it's especially scary for them to realize that their parents are scared.

Scary, Confusing Images

The way that news is presented on television can be quite confusing for a young child. The same video segment may be shown over and over again through the day, as if each showing was a different event. Someone who has died turns up alive and then dies again and again. Children often become very anxious since they don't understand much about videotape replays, close-ups, and camera angles. Any televised danger seems close to home to them because the tragic scenes are taking place on the television set right in their own living room. Children can't tell the difference between what's close and what's far away, what's real and what's pretend, or what's new and what's rerun.

The younger the children are, the more likely they are to be interested in scenes of close-up faces, particularly if the people are expressing strong feelings. When there's tragic news, the images on TV are most often much too graphic and disturbing for young children.

"Who will take care of me?"

In times of crisis, children want to know, "Who will take care of me?" They're dependent on adults for their survival and security. They're naturally self-centered. They need to hear very clearly that their parents are doing all they can to take care of them and to keep them safe. They also need to hear that people in the government and other grownups they don't even know are working hard to keep them safe, too.

Helping Children Feel More Secure

Play is one of the important ways young children have of dealing with their concerns. Of course, playing about violent news can be scary and sometimes unsafe, so adults need to be nearby to help redirect that kind of play into nurturing themes, such as a hospital for the wounded or a pretend meal for emergency workers.

When children are scared and anxious, they might become more dependent, clingy,

When I was a boy and I would see scary things in the news, my mother would say to me, "Look for the helpers. You will always find people who are helping." To this day, especially in times of "disaster," I remember my mother's words, and I am always comforted by realizing that there are still so many helpers—so many caring people in this world.

and afraid to go to bed at night. Whining, aggressive behavior, or toilet "accidents" may be their way of asking for more comfort from the important adults in their lives. Little by little, as we adults around them become more confident, hopeful, and secure, our children probably will too.

Turn Off the TV

When there's something tragic in the news, many parents get concerned about what and how to tell their children. It's even harder than usual if we're struggling with our own powerful feelings about what has happened. Adults are sometimes surprised that their own reactions to a televised crisis are so strong, but great loss and devastation in the news often reawaken our own earlier losses and fears—even some we thought we had "forgotten."

It's easy to allow ourselves to get drawn into watching televised news of a crisis for hours and hours; however, exposing ourselves to so many tragedies can make us feel hopeless, insecure, and even depressed. We help our children and ourselves if we're able to limit our own television viewing. Our children need us to spend time with them—away from the frightening images of on the screen.

Talking and Listening

Even if we wanted to, it would be impossible to give our children all the reasons for such things as war, terrorists, abuse, murders, fires, hurricanes, and earthquakes. If they ask questions, our best answer may be to ask them, "What do you think happened?" If the answer is "I don't know," then the simplest reply might be something like, "I'm sad about the news, and I'm worried. But I love you, and I'm here to care for you."

If we don't let children know it's okay to feel sad and scared, they may try to hide those feelings or think that something is wrong with them whenever they do feel that way. They certainly don't need to hear all the details of what's making us sad or scared, but if we can help them accept their own feelings as natural and normal, their feelings will be much more manageable for them.

Angry feelings are part of being human, especially when we feel powerless. One of the most important messages we can give our children is, "It's okay to be angry, but it's not okay to hurt ourselves or others." Besides giving children the right to their anger, we can encourage them to find constructive things to do with their feelings. This way, we'll be giving them useful tools that will serve them all their life, and help them to become the world's future peacemakers—the world's future "helpers."

Helpful Hints

■ Do your best to keep the television off, or at least limit how much your child sees of any news event.

■ Try to keep yourself calm. Your presence can help your child feel more secure.

■ Give your child extra comfort and physical affection, like hugs, or snuggling up together with a favorite book. Physical comfort goes a long way towards providing inner security. That closeness can nourish you, too.

■ Try to keep regular routines as normal as possible. Children *and* adults count on familiar patterns of everyday life.

■ Plan something that you and your child enjoy doing together, like taking a walk, going on a picnic, having some quiet time, or doing something silly. It can help to know there are simple things in life that can help us feel better, both in good times and in bad.

■ Even if children don't mention what they've seen or heard in the news, it can help to ask what they think has happened. If parents don't bring up the subject, children can be left with their own misinterpretations. You may be surprised at how much your child has heard from others.

■ Focus attention on the helpers, like the police, firemen, doctors, nurses, paramedics, and volunteers. It's reassuring to know that there are many caring people who are doing all they can to help others in this world.

■ Let your child know if you're making a donation, going to a town meeting, writing a letter or e-mail of support, or taking some other action. It can help children to know that adults take many different active roles, and that we don't give in to helplessness in times of worldwide crisis.

Divorce and Separation

"When I took my daughter to the park we happened to pass by a wishing well. She told me that ever since her father and I got divorced (which was several years ago), she always dropped a coin in a wishing well and made a wish that her father and I would get back together again. I didn't think she would hold on to that wish for such a long time!"

Divorce is sad and painful. During a separation or divorce, children often feel as if their family is "broken." They might even worry that, "Since my parents stopped loving each other, they might stop loving me." Divorce changes families in many ways. But it's still possible for children to feel secure, safe, and loved, even when their parents don't live together.

"Who will take care of me?"

Since young children are naturally egocentric (which comes from our human need to survive), they want to know, "Who will take care of me?" When children see their parents upset and overwhelmed by divorce, they often feel it's up to them to be the caregivers in the family. What a heavy burden that can be! It's reassuring for children to hear that grownups will continue to take care of them, and will continue to take care of themselves, as well.

"It's all my fault . . ."

One of the most common reactions to parents separating and divorcing is that children believe it's their fault. In fact, they often wonder if divorce might be a kind of punishment for times when they were "bad." They need to hear very clearly from adults that all children misbehave once in a while, and that divorce doesn't happen because of children's misbehavior. Divorce is a problem among *adults*.

Sometimes children feel that they're to blame for the divorce because they've had fantasies about getting rid of one of their parents. How scary it can be for them to discover that their fantasy life is so powerful that their wish has come true! We need to let children know that wishes don't make things come true—not good things *or* bad things.

Some children in a divorced family think that it's up to them to get their parents back together again. It's important to remind them that they didn't make the divorce happen in the first place and that they can't bring their parents back together either—not by wishing, not by being "a perfect child," not even by being a "perfectly unruly child." It's only parents who can make a decision about such an adult thing as a divorce.

Children's Right to Feel

Divorce is about loss—loss of the family as the child has known it, sometimes the loss of a familiar home. Often deep sadness and anger accompany such a loss. One thing we can always give our children is the right to feel— the right to feel sadness, anger, and pain. We can also do our best in giving them the security of knowing that they still have a family and adults in their life who will care for them and love them.

Parents' Needs and Feelings

When there's a separation or divorce, parents can be hurt and angry, too. Many parents talk about feeling overwhelmed by the new responsibilities of being a single parent, guilty about

*S*everal years ago, when we produced a television special about divorce, a woman in the studio audience stood up to tell us something that had been enormously helpful for her as a girl when her parents divorced. She said, "I will always be grateful to my mom because she encouraged my own loving feelings towards my dad. I knew mom didn't have those feelings, but she cared enough to let me have them and go on to build my own relationship with him." What strength that mother had—being able to separate her own needs from those of her daughter! And what a life-long gift it obviously has been for her daughter!

what the divorce will do to their children, and most of all, feeling like they are a terrible failure. But just because a marriage has failed doesn't mean that a husband and wife are failures. Divorced people can still be loving and lovable, in many ways.

Take Care of Yourself

It's very hard to have energy for the everyday needs of your child when you yourself are feeling hurt, upset, and unloved. One of the first ways to help your child is to offer some help to yourself. Try not to be too judgmental or demanding of yourself. Some people try to go through the hard times of divorce with a constant "stiff upper lip." Pretending that pain, anger, and sadness aren't there doesn't fool anyone. If you're having a hard day, you can let your children know it and assure them that they're not the cause. Feeling the pain and finding healthy ways to deal with our feelings are important parts of healing for adults as well as for children.

You know your child. If you sense that you or your child needs extra help, look for an appropriate counselor or support group. Some people think that needing professional help is a sign of weakness. Not so! It's usually strong people

and emotionally healthy people who are able to seek and accept help when they need it. What's more, everybody needs help sometimes. Anything that encourages you to remember that you are a lovable and loving person is worth your time and energy.

Divorce changes families in many ways. But a mother and father who don't live together can still cherish their children and help them feel secure, safe, and loved.

Helpful Hints

■ Young children don't need details about why parents are getting divorced. It's enough to say to them, "We are very, very sorry. We talked about it and worked at it, but we cannot live together anymore." Your child may not be able to "hear" what you're saying, particularly at stressful times, so you may have to say things again and again.

■ It's helpful for children if both parents can be there with them (if possible) when they're told about the divorce for the first time. They need to see that both parents

care about them and that both will continue to be their parents.

■ If the other parent isn't at all involved, you may be able to offer some comfort by letting your child know that some parents have such a difficult time with their feelings that they aren't able to show their love.

■ It can be very helpful to talk with your children about specific changes, like: where they will sleep or go to school, where each parent will live, when the children will be with each parent. Children who are left to wonder about those very basic things are likely to make up their own fantasy answers, which may be a lot scarier than the truth. Even when those details are uncertain, children can find comfort in knowing you're going to work them out.

■ Talk about the things that will stay the same, especially your love. Children want to know that some things will not change. They need to know there will still be rules. Rules help them feel secure and loved.

■ Children who feel powerful enough to think they have caused the divorce are especially in need of firm rules. Even though they may fight the rules, they really do feel more secure when they know that adults are in charge.

■ Continue to do things together that you and your child enjoy—even small things, like reading a book together, taking a walk, or going to a favorite sports event. It's reassuring for you and your child to know there still will be things to enjoy, even in hard times.

■ Encourage your child to use words like "I'm scared" or "I'm mad" or "I'm sad." That's so much better than lashing out at other people or damaging things. One of the most important uses of language is expressing feelings.

■ Suggest physical activity, like pounding play clay, running in the yard, digging in a pile of dirt, or playing at a playground, all of which can help your child drain off some of the tension of strong feelings. You could also encourage drawing pictures, talking to and for a puppet, or making up stories.

■ Read children's books about divorce together. Hearing about other children who are dealing with divorce and talking about pictures in a book can often encourage children to bring up their own feelings and concerns and know they are not alone.

■ No matter how different the situation, it's best not to say negative things about the other parent. Children feel much more secure when they can have positive relationships with both parents.

■ Children sometimes feel caught in the middle between parents. They worry they're betraying one parent when they like being with the other one, so they may not want to leave one parent to visit with the other. Just knowing you understand that it's hard for them can help those times be more manageable. "Children can love their moms *and* their dads even when they're divorced" can be so helpful to hear!

Stepfamilies

"My son spends weekends with his father and stepmother. A few months ago, I noticed that when he came back from being with them, he seemed uncomfortable when he talked about his stepmother. It was as if he was afraid to show me that he likes her. I decided to talk with him about that, and I told him it was okay with me if he likes her—that it didn't mean he didn't love me. I could see his whole body relax. I think he felt he was hurting me if he gave me any indication that there were things about her that he liked. He still doesn't talk much about her, but whenever does he seems a lot more comfortable."

Children bring many feelings and fantasies into a stepfamily. One of the hardest things in accepting a stepparent is that children first have to let go of the fantasy they've probably been holding onto since their parents were divorced—that their biological parents will marry each other again and put the original family back together. Seeing one of their parents get married to someone else starts to dissolve that dream, and the children are likely to feel resentful. No wonder a parent's wedding day can be a very hard time.

Difficult Changes

After a divorce or death of a parent, children naturally draw closer to and become more dependent on the parent who's still there. In fact, a child whose father has gone may see his or her mother as more "mine" than ever before. When a new parent steps in, that child has to share the "all mine mommy" again, and that can feel like another big loss.

Of course, new routines, new responsibilities, new expectations, sometimes a different home or sleeping arrangement can be very, very hard. When there are too many changes all at once, young children sometimes feel helpless, sad, and angry. They might even start to act like babies again or get to be overly demanding of their parent or their stepparent.

When new "brothers and sisters" come along with a new parent it's only natural that the original child could be jealous about who has more privileges, and who gets more attention from the biological parent and from the stepparent. Seeing a parent shower attention on stepchildren sometimes makes a child wonder, "Who do you love more? After all I'm *your* child!"

Complicated Feelings

Children can feel pulled between the old family and the new one. They might wonder, "Am I betraying my dad if I like my stepdad . . . or am I betraying my stepdad if I still love my dad?" They may also feel it's too much of a risk to develop an attachment with a stepparent, because some day that person might leave, too.

Jealousy, anger, fear, and sadness are natural and normal in all families and particularly in stepfamilies. What children need to know is that talking about and dealing with those feelings is part of the work that it takes to make the new family a real family.

Little by little, most children find their way through the complex feelings of living in a stepfamily. With help from their parents and stepparents, they can come to know that there's real security in loving relationships.

A couple that I know separated when their daughter was a baby. When she turned four, her mother remarried. Her mother told me, "My daughter had a very hard time accepting my new husband into our family. She would tell him she hated him and that she wanted him to go away. I think in her own way, she was testing my husband and me to see if he would really stay before she would allow herself to accept our new family. We let her know that we cared about her feelings, but we also told her clearly that my new husband was here to stay. She finally settled in, and I think it helped her to hear those messages."

It Takes Effort to Make a New Family

Most couples have high expectations, hopes, and dreams as they begin to establish their stepfamily. While there can be concern over how the children will adjust, the parents tend to be confident that their love will be strong enough to hold this new family together. Too often, though, couples start out life together without realizing how much effort it takes to make a healthy "blended family." They may also feel especially pressured because they don't want a second marriage to end in divorce.

Both partners bring into the marriage leftover feelings from the past and often very different perceptions of what family life together will be. Because the adults are looking forward to this new relationship as an extra special "second chance," it can be a real disappointment when they find that their children don't share in their joy.

When children are belligerent, argumentative, or withdrawn, it's hard for their parents to remember that those children are probably hurting. Most stepparents find that family life tends to be far smoother if they can balance children's needs with those of the adults.

Discipline

One of the biggest challenges for a stepparent is figuring out what role to take in disciplining. Effective discipline grows out of a healthy relationship between a parent and a child, and that relationship grows out of a history of nurturing, warm, and loving times.

It's understandable, then, that the biological parent is at first generally the more effective disciplinarian for his or her child. If there are times when the stepparent has to intervene, some children might say, "I don't have to listen to you! You're not my mom (or dad)!" They might even argue that there are different rules in the other parent's home. It's often best to say something like, "Different parents do things differently. And this is the way we do things here." It's helpful, therefore, to have firm rules that are clearly understood and that apply to all the children when they're in that particular household.

Relationships grow little by little, and they often thrive in "just you and me" times, when you're doing something together that you both enjoy, like making a snack, reading a book, or going to the playground.

In most stepfamilies, it takes years to build respectful, warm, and affectionate relationships—years of listening and talking about important things that help everyone in the family to grow together.

Helpful Hints

■ Try to include the children in some way in the wedding ceremony or in any gatherings afterward. Ask the children what they might like to do. It's okay if they don't want to be involved. You are helping them know they're important in the new family, just by your asking them.

■ If you're moving to a new home, whenever possible let the children make some decisions about their bedroom, like where to put the furniture or what color to paint the walls. That way, the room will feel more like their place.

■ If stepchildren come for weekends or short visits, set aside some space for them: a room or at least a drawer that is just theirs. Having a place of their own can help children feel much more welcome and secure.

■ Holidays can be especially hard because of the additional stepfamily obligations. Before the holidays, do your best to talk with your child about the plans and give some options.

■ Difficult feelings, fears, and fantasies may surface with further changes in the family, like before a baby is born or before the parents go away on a trip. At these times, children need extra support. They need to know that no one will ever take their unique place in your heart.

■ Try to establish some regularity in your child's contact with the other parent. If children know when they can count on a phone call or a visit, they have some time to get more comfortable and feel more in control. Most children (and adults!) would much rather know what to expect than to be surprised.

■ Whenever possible, do your best to help the children maintain their relationships with grandparents and other relatives of their biological family. They are a part of them and their history. When children feel connected to their past, they are much more likely to feel secure in the present.

■ Many stepfamilies find it helpful to have some professional counseling early on. It can be a challenge to know which problems are part of any family life and which might be due to the blending of families. There are many professionals who have a lot of experience with stepfamilies.

Dealing with Death

"In the first few days after my father died, I cried a lot. That really upset my daughter. She would beg me, 'Smile, Mommy, smile.' So I decided to try to hide my sadness. But my daughter seemed to know that I was really sad and on the verge of tears. I told her that even though she couldn't make my sadness go away, she could do something really important by comforting me with her hugs. I think her hugs helped her as much as they helped me."

Most young children know something about death. They may have seen a dead bird or bug or had a pet who died. Also, they may have seen people on television die. Still, their notion of death is very limited and simplistic, and they probably have many misunderstandings. It's precisely because children don't understand what death is about that they need help from loving adults in talking about it.

Children Are Curious

Children naturally know best what they can see or touch. Their earliest idea of death is that whatever is dead doesn't move. They can't comprehend much beyond that. They're curious about death, and they might ask questions like, "If we set Grandma up in the casket, what would happen?"

Many of children's concerns focus on body functions that are important to them—"Can a dead person or animal get hungry . . . feel cold . . . make a bm or pee-pee in the ground?" Children don't mean to be rude or hurt anybody's feelings with what they ask or say. They're just wondering about a lot of different things at the time of a death. Asking the same question again and again gives a child another chance to test our answers and gradually come to their own understanding.

Of course, the finality of death is the hardest thing to comprehend, particularly for young children. After all, their friends "play dead," then get up and run around again, and dead cartoon characters pop up alive again. A child whose mother had died asked, "Is Mommy coming back for my birthday?" It takes a long time for children to realize that death is permanent.

Children may also be curious to see what "dead" looks like. Some parents are concerned that seeing an open casket will traumatize their child. With caring preparation, seeing a dead body can be less frightening than the fantasies that many children have about it. Children may even want to touch the body to see "what dead feels like."

Words Can Be Confusing

Even though children respond more to the tone of our voice than to any particular words we use, it's important to be careful with our explanations. Children tend to take what we say literally. Someone once told a child that death was like "going to sleep." That child had great difficulty going to bed and getting to sleep because she was afraid she might not ever wake up. If children hear that someone has "lost" a father or a daughter, imagine what they

My first recollection of anyone close to me dying is from when I was six years old. My Grandfather Rogers worked as a plant engineer for a steel company and was a very strong man. He died suddenly of a heart attack. It had never occurred to me that such a strong person would ever die.

*What I remember most clearly about Grandfather Rogers' dying was my own father's crying. I saw Dad in the hallway with tears streaming down his face. I don't think I had ever seen him cry before. I'm glad I did see him, though, because many years later, when **he** died, I cried; and way down deep I knew that he would have said it was all right.*

might think! Or hearing that grandpa went on a "long, long journey," a child might want to know, "If he came home from his vacation last year, when will he come back this time?"

Despite our best intentions, many of our words can be frightening or confusing to children. "If heaven is up in the sky," some children have wondered, "Why are we burying Aunt Suzie in the ground?" Or, "If I go up in an airplane, can I see my baby sister who's in heaven?" When unknowing adults say, "Your daddy is in heaven watching over you," they usually mean to be reassuring, but to a child, those words might raise the image of a spy who sees and knows everything that the child thinks and does. It's often more helpful to answer a child's questions about death with, "No one knows for sure, but I believe . . ." Saying "I wonder about that, too," is also a special way of keeping the communication between parent and child open.

Each Child Reacts Differently

When a loved one has died, some children may cry a lot, while others may not. Some find it easy to talk openly, and others hold their thoughts and feelings inside for a long time. One child might find comfort in music, while another might turn to storybooks. Some may even act as though nothing has happened and go about their everyday business of playing as usual. It takes time for children to understand what death and dying means, and even when they do understand, they may not feel ready to acknowledge their painful feelings. Of course, it's important for us adults to honor that. Each one in the family has his or her own way of expressing grief, at his or her own pace.

Expressing Feelings

When children are four and five, their aggressive urges are often very strong. If a child happens to be angry with a parent, and that parent happens to die, the child could have a terrible struggle wondering how much of his or her anger is responsible for the parent's death. Children need to hear that no matter how much we love someone, there are times when we get angry with that person, and just because we have angry thoughts doesn't mean that we make somebody die. It's most important for children to realize that thoughts and wishes don't make things happen, whether they're good or bad things.

Children may be angry, too, because a person they love has died and left them. It can help to say to a child something like, "It can make a person really angry to have someone go away and not come back. Most people feel awful when someone they love dies." Just identifying a feeling and hearing that there's nothing wrong with it can be a big help to a child and can make it easier to talk more about it—then or later.

When children are going through stressful times, they often regress to a time that was safer. They also tend to lose abilities they've already achieved, like toilet training, talking clearly, and sleeping through the night. They may even become clingy, whiny, and overly dependent, demanding attention in whatever way they can get it.

One of the most appropriate and necessary ways that children grieve is through their play. Some parents are uncomfortable when their children "play" about death right after a family member has died. Those parents may feel that it shows that the child is insensitive. But just the opposite is true. Children who play about death are usually feeling *so* sensitive about it that they're using the best means they have to try to come to terms with what it means and how they feel about it.

Parents' Needs and Feelings

When someone we care about dies, we adults may feel so empty that we haven't much desire to think about anything except what has happened to us. It's only natural to think that we haven't much to give to anyone else, and yet, at a time like this, our children need us more than ever.

It can be hard to know just what children do need at such times, but very often the same things that help us will help them, too—simple things, like hugging, talking, and having quiet times together. Inviting and including our children in our own traditional family ways of coping with grief is one of the best things we can do for our children and for ourselves. It's easy to forget that children can be having some of the same feelings we're having—sadness, loneliness, even anger and guilt. Knowing that those feelings are natural and normal for *all* of us can make it easier to share them with each other.

Responding to Children's Questions

Your child may hear of someone's death in another family and suddenly realize that people do die. Sooner or later, most children ask, "Will you die, Mommy . . . Daddy?" With honesty and confidence, we can say something like "I hope to be alive for a long, long time. And no matter what, there will always be someone to take care of you."

Death is a mystery. When children ask questions about death, nobody has all the answers. Even if you have said something that you later regret, let your child know that you thought of a better way to talk about it. If you can accept your humanness, your child can, too.

There will probably be many times throughout their lives when children will feel that the world has turned upside-down. Knowing that real love and good memories never die can nourish everyone in the family in every time of need.

Helpful Hints

Talking about Death:

■ It helps to use examples with words that children can understand like "the dead fish can't move or eat or swim—ever again."

■ Burying a dead goldfish in the yard gives you a chance to say that when bodies are dead they are often buried in the ground. If we have prepared our children for death before an important human being in their life dies, they may be better able to cope when that time comes.

■ Share your memories of your experiences and feelings when you were a child and a loved pet or person died. That gives your child an important way of knowing that feelings are natural and normal.

■ It's frightening for children to think that the sadness they feel when someone they love dies may overwhelm them and never go away. There can be real comfort in hearing that "sadness doesn't last forever" and "the very same people who are sad sometimes are the very same people who are glad sometimes"—and that it's true for all of us. It also gives them permission to laugh and have fun if that's what they feel. Enjoying something isn't a betrayal of the loved one's memory. It's a way to honor the loved one by appreciating life.

■ While it may seem that, for the moment, you've put your child's questions about death to rest, something may trigger the same or different questions later on. As with most challenging things in life, you'll have many opportunities to help your children work through what death means to them.

■ You may want to encourage your child to make a photo album or a story book with memories of the person who died. It's one way to keep the memories alive in us and to keep the relationship alive in our hearts and minds. Grieving isn't about forgetting. It's about coming to accept the death little by little and finding ways to enrich our family by continuing to remember our relationship with the person who has died.

■ It can help to spend some quiet time with your child doing something together that you both enjoy, like reading a book or taking a walk. Adults and children who are grieving need extra comfort and attention, and those moments of being together can nourish both you and your child. If it means temporarily changing some of the routines, you'll sense the best time to help your child gradually get back to "normal."

■ When a mother, father, sibling, or any other very close relative or friend dies, that can be one of the most difficult tragedies for any family to face. If you feel that you or your child needs professional help in living through such a tough time, look for a grieving counselor or support group. There are grieving centers that offer important support and information for families with young children.

The Funeral:
■ Even very young children can benefit from participating in at least some of the rituals that attend death, so long as we prepare them for what to expect and can listen to their questions. Feeling excluded is much harder for children than feeling sad.

■ Before going to the funeral, let your child know that there may be people crying. Mention, too, that there may also be people chattering away and even telling humorous stories. Help your child know that each person deals with death and funerals in his or her own way.

■ If you take your child to the funeral home, you might want to have an adult friend (with whom your child is comfortable) stay close at hand. That friend can help if your child needs to take a break, go to the bathroom, or gets upset by the crying, crowds, or commotion.

■ If your child really doesn't want to go to the actual funeral, or if your own needs are such that you don't feel that you can take your child along, there are other ways he or she can be included in this important time of grieving. You might arrange for a special "family only" time with you at the funeral home or cemetery, or suggest that your child help after the funeral by greeting guests or helping to serve whatever refreshments there might be.

■ If your child is willing, just having him or her on your lap during the funeral service can give comfort to you, too. Having children nearby at a time like this reminds us that life goes on and on and on.

MISTER ROGERS'

PLAY TIME

**Encourage Your Child to Create,
Explore, and Pretend with Dozens
of Easy-to-Do Activities**

by Fred Rogers

Our Thanks to . . .

One of the fortunate things about growing up during the "B.T." (Before Television) era is that I spent much of my childhood playing about all sorts of things. The work on this book has its roots not only in my love of play but also in the appreciation that my parents and grandparents, neighbors and friends had for the everyday playtimes of their childhoods. Healthy, happy childhoods have many, many playtimes.

For me, one of the joys of being a father and a grandfather is being involved in the ways that my sons and grandsons play. I'm grateful to them for giving me another chance to grow in understanding what play can mean to everyone in the family.

During the years that I studied child development, I came to honor play as the "work" of children through my mentors, Dr. Margaret McFarland, Dr. Albert Corrado, and Dr. Nancy Curry. I'm especially thankful for the generous sharing of their insight, their delight, their fascination with the ways that children use play as they grow and learn—and the essential role of the encouraging adult in their development.

Turning our love of playtime into a book for parents became the work of two of our longtime staff members, Hedda Bluestone Sharapan and Cathy Cohen Droz. Their passion for play and their genuine care for the families who would use this book were obvious throughout this project. As I've come to know them and their own families over the years, it's been obvious that they are both parents who value playtime with their own children and who enjoy playfulness in everyday life. Hedda and Cathy love fun, and they obviously love to help others discover it, too. How grateful I am to know them well!

Thanks, too, to our consultant, Dr. Roberta Schomburg, and to a previous staff member and friend, Barry Head, who, through their earlier work with us, have provided an enormous wealth of activities that could inform this present work. We're grateful to Karin Haug, our summer intern, who brought a fresh approach to our discussions. And thanks also to one of our staff members, Britanny Loggi-Smith, and her family, who graciously offered to follow some of the recipes and activities to ensure that our directions were clear and accurate. What's more, they shared the "fruits" of their cooking with all of us at Family Communications, Inc.—delicious!

Our friends at Running Press, especially Melissa Wagner, our editor, and Alicia Freile, our designer, gave their careful, caring attention as we all worked together to make this a helpful book for families. And we were especially pleased to have been able to work again with an old friend, Maureen Rupprecht, who illustrated this book with her usual sensitive artistry.

Everyone at our small nonprofit company, Family Communications, Inc., has contributed in some way to this book, as they do with all our projects. Their dedication in helping provide what's meaningful for children and their pleasure in the playfulness of the lives of their families is an on-going inspiration to me. We all hope that you and your children will continue to delight in growing through the playtimes of your lives.

Introduction

" Child's play" is one of the most misleading phrases in our language. People often use it to suggest something trivial, but a child's play is not trivial—not by any means. When children play, they're working. They're working on learning about themselves, about other people, and about the world around them. Playtime is one of the most important times for children to learn and grow.

When I watch children play, I get particular pleasure from seeing them use whatever they have to play with in unexpected ways. A child who uses an empty wrapping paper tube as a tunnel for little cars to go through, or a towel for a teddy bear's blanket, is a creative child, a discoverer, and a problem-solver. Playtime in childhood can be the root of lifelong abilities that help us to cope, to learn, and to become all that we can be.

Playtime for learning—and fun

A letter came to us a while ago that said so much to me about playtime and parenting.

"I'm a 28-year-old mother. I've been feeling the responsibility of being a parent very heavily. . . . So I've bought books and books and books. I felt sure that if I didn't do exactly right as a parent, my son would suffer. By his second birthday, I made sure he could count to twelve and recognize all the letters of the alphabet.

". . . I've since come to realize that my son needed to be a child, and that I needed him to be one. Now that means more to me than trying to store information in his ever-expanding brain. It means letting him enjoy life as only a child can, with the sheer enjoyment of the wonders of this world, however small they may be. Did you know you can see rainbows on the wings of common houseflies?

"This afternoon my son and I pretended to be different kinds of animals, laughing a lot. Then we got tired, so we sat at the table and made a pinwheel. My son didn't learn about the ABCs or numbers, but he was learning to pretend and play for fun."

I would venture a guess that, at the same time, her son was learning all sorts of important things—things that would help him in school, like imagination, sticking to a task, following directions, paying attention—and feeling good about himself and his relationship with others.

She continued in her letter,

"At last I feel like I've been given permission to be the kind of parent I want to be. I'm not a teacher. I'm a mom, and an imperfect mom at that, with fears and hopes and dreams like anyone else—but with an awful lot of love inside for my little boy."

Her comments reminded me of something essential that I learned from Helen Ross, a remarkable teacher in child development and a consultant for the *Neighborhood* programs—DON'T FORGET THE FUN!

About this book

Besides offering fun and meaningful activities, we wanted to make this book easy for parents to use. We've organized the activities in chapters, using categories that are of interest to children or characteristics that parents want to encourage.

In every chapter we've offered a variety of activities—ideas for what to do with food, crafts, music, movement, and outdoor play. You know your child best, so you're the best one to decide which activities your child might enjoy.

You might also want to use the index in which we've listed each type of activity. For example, if it's a nice day for outdoor playtime, you'll find the outside activities listed together in the index. Or, if it's a rainy day, you may want to look in the index to find a kitchen or craft idea.

When we made our selections for this book, we particularly kept in mind how busy parents are these days. We specifically chose ideas that take little preparation, are easy for children to do, and require only readily available household materials.

Some children may need extra help getting started, so we've included some suggestions. For example, if your child is stumped about what kind of picture to draw or dance to create, you could say, "How about 'one of your favorite places?'" or "a terrible day?" or "the best birthday party?" When we encourage children to bring something relevant from their own lives to their play, we're helping them reach into their uniqueness and express something that's meaningful for them.

Getting started

Start with what your child enjoys doing. Does your child spend a lot of time playing with toy cars? Maybe he or she likes to explore things outdoors. Or maybe you have a child who always seems to reach for a pencil or crayon to draw things. Turn to the chapters that feel like a good fit for your child.

You could also start with what you want to encourage in your child, like cooperation, help with chores around the house, talking about feelings, or developing an appreciation for nature.

You might want to look for the kind of play you like to do, too. What did you enjoy as a

child? Which chapter of this book catches your eye? Your enthusiasm for a particular kind of play will most likely make it more attractive for your child.

During one of my first practicum courses in Child Development at the University of Pittsburgh, I saw firsthand how much children's play can be affected by an adult. I was observing four-year-olds at the Family and Children's Center. The director of the center had invited a well-known sculptor to come to visit. The director said to the sculptor, "I'd like you simply to love working with your clay in front of the children—not teach them technique. Just love what you do in front of them." Well, that sculptor did just that, and little by little, those four year olds started doing their own unique things with clay—not as an assignment, but because they caught the notion that they could find satisfaction in using clay just as their guest did. That sculptor came to visit those young children once a week for the whole semester. Not before or since have that center's four-year-olds used the medium of clay so imaginatively.

That story reminds me of the Quaker saying, "Attitudes are caught, not taught." When you do with your child whatever you love to do, or even when you just talk about those things with your heartfelt appreciation, that's contagious!

Setting limits

When we introduce a playtime idea to a child, we often need to provide some limits, especially if we're indoors or in our homes. No one wants furniture or walls messed up.

Before you start the play, it's a good idea to let your child know about the rules, like "newspaper goes on the table before you paint" or "the clay stays on the table." Putting play clay on a cookie sheet might even be more helpful, so your child sees and feels where the clay needs to stay.

It can also help if you remind your child before you start playing that there will be clean-up time afterward. Then about ten minutes before you need to end the play, let your child know clean-up is coming soon. Clean-up time is a natural part of playtime.

There can be wonderful benefits, too, when we make limits on what our children can do. I remember watching a toddler whose mother had just told her to stop putting a pen into her mouth. From the look on the little girl's face, you could see she had a problem: how to please her mother and yet satisfy her urge to play with the pen. She solved her problem by finding a hole in the side of a toy—and for several minutes she played contentedly, poking the pen through the hole, dropping it, picking it up, and poking it through again.

Watching that happen helped me realize how important limits are for the development of children's creativity. When we won't let them do exactly what they want to do, they have the opportunity of creating new alternatives.

Parents and playtime

How much or how little you get involved in these activities depends on you, on your child's needs and abilities, and on the situation. For some of these activities and for some children, you may need only to set out the materials. The play will take hold, and you can step back.

When you're more involved, you're likely to find that it's more than "playtime" that happens. A friend of mine was sitting at the kitchen table and spotted an empty egg carton on the counter. He decided to make something from it that he remembered from his own childhood. His four-year-old daughter was in the next room, watching television, but at one point she wandered into the kitchen to see what was going on.

She asked her father what he was doing, and he told her, "I thought I'd see if I could make a toy car." When she asked, "Why?" he answered, "Just for fun. I used to make them from egg cartons when I was a boy."

She thought about that for a moment and asked if she could help. Her father invited her to sit by him and told her he could use some help. Half an hour went by, and little by little, the father helped his daughter do as much of the project as she was able to do. When it was done, she picked up the egg-carton car and ran upstairs to her mother and cried out, "Look, Mommy! Look what Daddy and I just made!" Just think about how much it meant to her—on many levels—to have that playtime with her father, building something together, appreciating each other's creative ideas, and feeling proud of what they made. And think about how much that playtime must have meant to her father, too!

Whenever you become involved, whether you're watching the play as an interested bystander or becoming a partner with your child in the play, you'll have a wonderful opportunity to learn more about your child— and probably more about yourself, too.

You may also find that by watching your child at play, you'll tap into some of the playfulness inside you, remembering your childhood and discovering new things about yourself. Parenting gives us many chances to grow right along with our growing children.

Sharing
and Caring

Encouraging cooperation and kindness

Sharing and caring go hand in hand. They're both hard for most children, but that doesn't mean those children are spoiled or uncooperative or unkind. It just means that they're human.

Friends of mine told me a story about something that happened on a day when their daughter Michelle had a friend over for the afternoon. The girls wanted to play outside, but the afternoon air was cool. Michelle threw a tantrum after her parents offered one of her sweaters to the friend. It wasn't a particular favorite of Michelle's, so they couldn't understand why she made such a fuss! They seemed to be asking me, "How did we raise such a selfish kid?"

Michelle's angry response to her parents' lending her sweater to her playmate was not unusual, and it was not the mark of an uncaring child. Most children have trouble sharing. Being able to share and to care happens through a long process. Even though we can't expect most preschoolers will always share, cooperate, and care about other people's feelings, there are things that we can do to encourage them in that direction.

Sharing from children's perspective

First, we can try to understand what sharing means from their point of view. To a young child, what's "me" is "mine" and what's "mine" is "me." You've probably heard a child say "me chair," instead of "my chair." No wonder it's hard for them to share—if sharing means giving up a part of "me."

A mother of a preschooler found that when her son was in control of when and what he would share, he was much more receptive to sharing his toys. The mother suggested to her son that he allow a friend to play with a certain toy when he was finished with it, and usually found that her son would hand over the toy after only a few moments more. I have a hunch that children are much more willing to "share" when they feel they're in control.

A kitchen timer is another way some parents help their children with taking turns. A timer is a neutral timekeeper, so children trust that when they give up a toy to another child, they will get it back after a certain amount of time.

Holding on vs. letting go

Before children can let go of something to share it, they need to know what it means to hold on to something, or own it. That's why it can help children to have some things that they don't have to share, like their favorite soft animal or blanket. Before a friend comes to play, it may be a good idea to let your child decide which toys he or she will be willing to let someone else play with. You might want to suggest that your child put away the toys that are just too personal to share.

One of the most difficult things for children to share is the attention of their parents, but when children can trust they will have their parents' undivided attention, even for a little bit of time each day, they are more likely to be able to share their parents at other times.

Developing empathy

Caring, too, grows little by little as children develop the ability to see the world through other people's eyes. That's the foundation for empathy, the capacity to appreciate how others might feel.

We can help children become more aware of others' needs by praising them when they share a toy or a snack or when they comfort someone who is hurt or crying. It helps to be on the look-out for such times. Your actions help your child to know that you appreciate such expressions of kindness. When you say to your child "You're really growing," you're helping to make it clear that we grow inside as well as outside.

Another thing we can do is to offer activities, like the ones in this chapter, that let children know first-hand that there's fun and value in sharing and caring. They'll learn, little by little, that great good comes from both.

Paper Chains

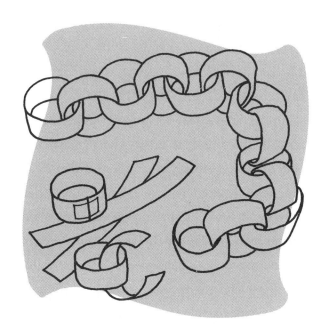

One child working alone can't make a very long chain, but if another child gets involved, that chain will grow . . . and grow . . . and grow!

YOU'LL NEED:
Assortment of colored construction paper
Blunt-nosed scissors
Glue or tape

✳ Show the children how to cut the construction paper into strips suitable for making small loops. Make a loop from a construction paper strip and tape or glue it together. Then show the children how to thread a second loop through the first to make a chain. The children might enjoy the challenge of making the chain as long as the whole room.

✳ When the chain is finished, hang it up with masking tape, and you've got a homemade decoration for a birthday or holiday—or a way to make an ordinary day all the more festive.

YOUR CHILD IS WORKING ON:
Teamwork
Dexterity

A Silly Folded Picture

Here's an idea that's no fun to do alone—your child will need at least one other partner, but it works even better with three.

YOU'LL NEED:
Sheets of paper
Pencil, pen, or marker

✳ Fold a sheet of paper in thirds, so that only the top third is showing.

✳ Out of view of the others, have your child draw the head of an animal or person on the top third. Then ask your child to fold that section under to hide what he or she has drawn.

✳ The next person sees only the middle third, where he or she will draw the body of the person or animal. Fold the picture so the top two-thirds are hidden, and pass it on to someone else.

✳ The last person will draw the legs of the animal or person.

✳ Unfold the picture to find a funny group masterpiece!

YOUR CHILD IS WORKING ON:
Appreciating other people's ideas
Dexterity
Imagination

Taking Turns

Like most games, this one gives children practice at taking turns. Since it also involves reading words and numbers, the children will probably need help from you or an older child.

YOU'LL NEED:
Blunt-nosed scissors
Cardboard or heavy paper
Brass paper fastener
Marker
Paper or index cards

Make a spinner: Cut a 5- or 6-inch circle or square from cardboard or heavy paper and divide it into sections, writing a number in each section. Make a 3-inch arrow from the leftover cardboard and attach it to the circle using a brass paper fastener. Loosen the arrow if necessary so it spins easily.

✳ Cut paper into 3 x 5-inch pieces to use as instruction cards. Ask the children to think of activities to write on the cards. Here are a few suggestions:

> Clap your hands
> Whisper "no, thank you"
> Turn around
> Touch your toes
> Shout "yes, please"
> Say your name
> Knock on the door

✳ Mix up the cards. Have a child pick a card, then spin the spinner to see how many times to do what the card says. For example, if the spinner stops on four and the card says "Say your name," the child will say his or her name four times.

YOUR CHILD IS WORKING ON:
Taking turns
Patience
Literacy
Number recognition

A Clothespin Cooperation Game

With this game, children can see that some things can't get accomplished unless they work together.

YOU'LL NEED:
3 or 4 clothespins (the spring type)
String, yarn, or clothesline
Plastic milk jug with a narrow opening

✳ Tie pieces of yarn onto the clothespins (one for each child) and put the clothespins inside the milk jug with only the strings hanging out.

✳ Tell the children to pull the clothespins from the jar. What happens if they all try to pull at the same time? Can they think of a way to get the clothespins out?

YOUR CHILD IS WORKING ON:
Cooperation
Taking turns
Patience
Dexterity

This activity can open the door for discussions about other times when children need to cooperate. For example, what can they do when two children want the same cup? What if they want to play with the same toy? How can they solve those kinds of problems peacefully?

Room to Share

When you unfurl a long roll of paper and show the children they have a big area to draw on, they'll realize that they can work side by side and end up with a much bigger and more interesting mural than any one child can draw alone.

YOU'LL NEED:

A long piece of paper from a roll of plain
   shelf paper
Markers or crayons
Tape

✳ Unroll the paper to the length of the work
   area (the floor or a table). You'll probably
   need to use tape to hold the ends down.

✳ Help the children decide how to work
   together by asking questions like:

> How can we decide where each
>   person should draw?
> Should each person draw a part of
>   one picture, or should each draw
>   his or her own picture?
> Do they want to use a theme?
>   Maybe the ocean, a garden, the
>   circus, or a house and yard?

✳ Once the children have come to an agree-
   ment, set out the crayons or markers, and
   let them get to work.

✳ This could be a fun way to make a birthday
   banner for a friend or for someone in the
   family. What an interesting way to say
   "we care about you."

YOUR CHILD IS WORKING ON:
Cooperation
Creativity
Decision-making
Appreciating other people's ideas

> **Be sure to comment with an encourag-
> ing word when the children are work-
> ing well together. They probably aren't
> going to get along all the time, but
> when you praise the cooperative
> moments, you're helping your child
> know you value cooperation.**

Fishing for Words

Watch your child practice taking turns, work on imagination and dexterity, and appreciate reading while playing this fishing game with one or more friends.

YOU'LL NEED:
Magnet
String
Pencil or ruler
Fish shapes cut from heavy paper
Paper clips
Bucket or dish pan

✳ Tie a magnet to a piece of string, then fasten the string to a pencil or ruler to make a fishing rod.

✳ Your child may be able to help draw or cut fish shapes from heavy paper and place paper clips on them.

✳ On each fish, write an activity for your child to do. Here are some suggestions for pretending:

Pretend to be a baby
Pretend to walk like a very tall person
Pretend to be an animal
Pretend to be a dancer

✳ Put all of the fish into the bucket or dish pan. Have the children try to catch the fish with the rod—it might take a while to get one. When a child's rod catches a fish, he or she does the activity written on the fish, and then waits for his or her next turn while the other children go fishing.

YOUR CHILD IS WORKING ON:
Taking turns
Persistence
Patience
Pretending
Literacy

A Pizza Factory

Here's a meal that can be done as an assembly line, with everyone sharing in the work.

YOU'LL NEED:
Bagels or English muffins (cut or split in half)
Bowls for toppings
Tomato sauce
Mozzarella cheese slices
Pizza toppings (i.e. mushrooms, olive slices, green peppers, etc.)
Mixing spoon
Cookie sheet

✳ Lay out the ingredients in a line on the table, so that each child will have his or her own work space.

✳ With input from the children, decide who will do the tasks that will be necessary to make the individual pizzas, including:

> Spread the sauce
> Tear the cheese into shreds
> Put the cheese onto the pizzas
> Put on the additional toppings
> Put the pizzas on to the cookie sheet

✳ Let the children know that for safety reasons, an adult needs to be the one to put the cookie sheet under the broiler or in a toaster oven. The pizzas are done when the cheese melts.

✳ Once the pizzas are ready, everyone can enjoy the fruits of their labor, thanks to the cooperation of the assembly line!

YOUR CHILD IS WORKING ON:
Teamwork
Dexterity
Making healthy food choices

A Caring Center

For young children, it can be such a good feeling to be the one who's giving the care.

YOU'LL NEED:
Baby dolls or stuffed animals
Small blankets or towels
Dress-up clothes (vest, purse, briefcase, tie)
Doll clothes (optional)
Baby bottle or spoon (optional)
Washcloths and masking tape for diapers

✳ Getting the play started probably won't take much more than stuffed animals or baby dolls and something that's like a blanket. Some children like to dress-up when they play mommies and daddies. For them, you might want to bring out grownup play-clothes, like vests, ties, aprons, purses, briefcases, etc. You might also make a swinging cradle by tying or pinning a sheet between two chairs.

✳ If the children need help getting started, you can ask what kinds of things mothers and fathers do to help take care of a baby— holding and rocking the baby; feeding the baby; changing the baby's diaper; telling the baby nursery rhymes; playing peek-a-boo; showing the baby rattles or toys.

✳ Think about how much it can mean to your child when you say something like, "Your baby is lucky to have such a caring parent."

YOUR CHILD IS WORKING ON:
Kindness
Developing a nurturing attitude
Role-playing

> **When children play about being care-givers for dolls or stuffed animals, they practice thinking of others' needs and doing specific tasks to care for them. Children are likely to take that good feeling of caring into everyday life.**

Mirror Images

Preschoolers are naturally egocentric, but in this activity they need to focus on another person's face, gestures, and movements. Your child's partner can be another child or an adult.

YOU'LL NEED:
A partner

✳ Have the partners stand in pairs, facing each other—as if they're looking in a mirror.

✳ One person starts as the leader. As the leader moves, the follower imitates that movement.

✳ At some point, change roles, so that each partner has the chance to be leader and follower.

YOUR CHILD IS WORKING ON:
Empathy
Observation skills
Taking turns
Coordination

In times of conflict, when your child has done something that upsets a friend, you could ask your child to look at his or her friend's face, just like your child did for this activity. Paying attention to other people's facial expressions or movements can help children realize that the things they do really affect others.

Thank-You Cards

"Thank you" may well be the most important phrase in the English language! Help your child develop an attitude of gratitude with this activity.

YOU'LL NEED:
Paper or an index card
Pencils, markers, or crayons
Magazine pictures or stickers (optional)
Glue (optional)
Envelope

✳ Fold the paper or index card in half to make a card.

✳ With your help, have your child think about someone who has done something nice or helpful for him or her. The card could be addressed to:

> Parent, brother, or sister
> Grandparent, neighbor, or friend
> Babysitter, child-care provider,
>   or preschool teacher
> Mail carrier
> Crossing guard

✳ Ask your child what kind of thank you message he or she would like to write in the card. A younger child might dictate the words to you. Older children may be able to write a message or sign their own names.

✳ Have your child decorate the front of the card with a drawing, magazine pictures, or stickers.

YOUR CHILD IS WORKING ON:
Expression of appreciation to others
Creativity
Literacy
Dexterity

Pretend Play

Developing imagination

A preschooler we know spent much of his playtime pretending to be a superhero. He was small for his age, spoke in a quiet voice, and was often shy when he met someone new, but once he had his cape on, he talked with a deep, strong voice, and he walked with a swagger. Just how much that costume meant to him became obvious to his family when he insisted on wearing his cape to the doctor's office. It seemed to help him feel braver and stronger—and made his visit to the doctor more manageable.

When children pretend, they aren't limited to the way things are in the real world. They're using their imagination to move beyond the bounds of reality. A stick can be a magic wand. A sock can be a puppet. A small child can be a powerful superhero, a crying baby, a mean dragon, or a scary lion—whatever he or she wants to be.

Trying on feelings

Although pretending can take many different forms, much of it seems to be a way for children to find out how they feel about something. Playing out different roles is a way for children to begin to understand other people's feelings, too. Seeing things from another person's point of view can be particularly hard for young children. Role playing can help them feel what it may be like to be another person for a little while.

Power and independence

One of the fascinating things about growing is how we move from dependence to independence. How dependent and independent children are—and how dependent and independent they want to be—is one of the biggest struggles of our earliest years. While children are often arguing about wanting to be in complete charge, they really don't want to be in charge because it would be too scary for them. Nevertheless, they can play about being in charge. In their play, children can put their toys and pretend people in different situations and make them act in ways they can't control real people or real big things around them. They play "all grown up!" Don't be surprised, though, if in the next moment they're playing about being the baby!

Understanding what's real and what's pretend

Sometimes pretending can seem so real that children wonder if putting on a costume might actually change them inside. It's important for them to know that although we can pretend to be someone else, we can never be someone else. We will always be ourselves.

Encouraging imagination

Whenever you encourage your child's imagination, you're also stretching your child's thinking skills. Young children know best what they see, hear, smell, or touch. That's concrete thinking. But when they use their imagination for their pretend play, they're using abstract thinking, and that's essential for school learning and for creative thinking and problem-solving all through life.

Parents sometimes wonder how much they ought to offer or suggest to stimulate imagination. The best kind of playthings are open-ended materials, like dress-up clothes, puppets, and art materials, because children can use them to work through their thoughts and feelings about the world. Some children need specific play props at times, like a toy telephone. Others may be satisfied if you just put your hand to your ear, pretending to talk on the phone. As you become an active partner in your child's imaginary play, you will come to know your child better, and you'll have a better sense of what might be helpful.

Grown-Up Play

Children especially like to imagine what it's like to be the grownups who are important in their lives—that's why they often play about being moms and dads.

YOU'LL NEED:
Any or all of the following:
- Purses
- Jewelry
- Hats
- Old briefcase
- Old nightgown
- Baby doll
- Baby bottle
- Blanket

YOUR CHILD IS WORKING ON:
Role-playing
Playing about power
Developing a nurturing attitude

✳ Some children see dress-up clothes and props and they immediately begin elaborate pretend play. Other children may need some help getting started. You might suggest a situation close to what your child has experienced. For example, pretend that there is a sick baby in the house or your child is a new babysitter who needs to learn the baby's routine. Familiar themes like that can make the best starters for dramatic play.

> While some children want to play about being the grownups, other children might want to be the babies. Sometimes the stresses of growing are hard, and children like to have a break by pretending to be the baby, wanting someone to take care of them.

Cape Play

Just putting on a cape can be enough of a prop to help your child play about all sorts of powerful roles: a king or queen or superhero.

YOU'LL NEED:
Soft blanket, large scrap of fabric, or a
   big towel
Large safety pin
Crown, jewelry (optional)
Magic wand (optional)
Deck of cards (optional)

✳ Pin the blanket, fabric, or towel loosely around your child's neck. What kind of play does the cape start for your child? You might suggest one of the following scenarios:

Royal Play: Your child might want to be a king or queen and plan a royal banquet for a meal. Show your child how to bow or curtsy to the guests (who might be friends, relatives, or even stuffed animals!). How might people eat in a fancy way? What might they say to each other? You might want to play some majestic sounding music, like Tchaikovsky's or Prokofiev's *Romeo and Juliet* ballets. Your child might enjoy commanding his or her "subjects" to do certain things—especially if you're the one who is pretending to obey his or her commands.

Superhero Play: Being powerful superheroes can be especially enticing play as children become more independent, yet still recognize that grownups control when they go to bed, when and what they eat, etc. This kind of play sometimes leads to chase-and-rescue running that can get out of hand. It can help your child to know ahead of time that you'll stop the play if someone might get hurt.

YOUR CHILD IS WORKING ON:
Using play to work on feeling powerful
Understanding the difference between
   real and pretend

Abracadabra

Some children delight in playing the role of a magician.

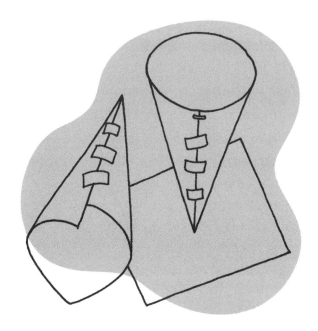

YOU'LL NEED:
Large sheet of black paper
Tape
Stapler
Blunt-nosed scissors
Strip of cardboard or stick
Glue
Glitter
Black cape, dark towel, or material (optional)

＊ To make a magician's hat, roll the paper into a cone shape with a point at one end. Tape the pointed end together and staple the bottom edge to fit your child's head. Cut off the extra paper at the bottom to make a straight edge.

＊ Make a magic wand by gluing glitter to the end of a strip of cardboard or stick.

＊ You might also want to offer a black cape, or a piece of black material or a dark towel to use as a cape.

＊ Your child might want to do pretend magic tricks. So much of the world is magical to young children. The very simplest "disappearing" tricks can be fun, and sometimes just pretending to have magical powers can be enough.

YOUR CHILD IS WORKING ON:
Playing about power
Understanding the difference between
   real and pretend

I Crown Thee King or Queen

Royal robes and glittery crowns can make your child feel grand, powerful, and very fancy.

YOU'LL NEED:
Strips of construction paper or lightweight cardboard about 4"–8" wide

Blunt-nosed scissors

Scrap craft materials (feathers, yarn, buttons)

Aluminum foil

Foil wrapping paper or metallic ribbon

Sequins or glitter (optional)

Glue

Tape

Majestic music (optional)

Food for a royal feast (optional)

＊ Tape two strips of paper together to make a crown that fits your child's head.

＊ Your child may need help cutting points or fringe along the top of the crown. Then your child can decorate with scrap materials, markers, small pieces of aluminum foil, foil wrapping paper, or metallic ribbon. Your child might also want to glue on sequins or sprinkle glitter over glue that has been drizzled on the crown.

＊ Fasten the headband around your child's head.

＊ Once your child is bedecked in these fancy things, you might want to greet him or her with a curtsy or bow, play some majestic music for a dance, or offer a feast to be eaten with royal table manners.

YOUR CHILD IS WORKING ON:
Feeling powerful

Developing imagination

Creativity

Pretending

An Imaginary Land

Here's imaginary play that starts with just one simple prop, a key, so you can do this anywhere—in the car, in a waiting room, or at home on a rainy day.

YOU'LL NEED:
Key or a key made out of cardboard

❋ Give your child the key and say something like "Let's pretend this key opens the door to an imaginary land." Let your child pretend to open a door with the key.

❋ You could ask questions like: What do you see when you open the door? Who is meeting you and taking you on a tour of this imaginary land? What is happening there?

YOUR CHILD IS WORKING ON:
Imagination
Pretending

As an active partner in this kind of imaginary play, you can encourage your child to rely more and more on his or her own imagination. It's hard for parents to know how much to elaborate. The more your child does, the less you'll need to do. Talking about imaginary things might remind you of your own childhood, and your child will probably love to hear about that.

What's Cooking?

With a chef hat and play dough or paper, your child can pretend to whip up a fabulous meal or dessert.

YOU'LL NEED:
20" x 30" piece of tissue or
   construction paper
Glue or staples
Cardboard strip 2" wide and just
   a little longer than the circumference
   of your child's head
Construction paper
Blunt-nosed scissors
Paper plates
Crayons or colored markers
Play clay (see recipe on page 92)

✳ Pleat a piece of tissue or construction paper and glue the pleated edge to the cardboard.

✳ Join the cardboard band and the pleated paper with glue or staples.

✳ Close the top of the hat by gluing a 3-inch circle of construction paper to the open sides of the crepe paper.

✳ Your child might want to use the play clay or construction paper to make pretend food like burgers, cakes, or cookies.

YOUR CHILD IS WORKING ON:
Creativity
Role-playing
Following directions

Paper Bag Hats

Save those paper bags—they make
great-looking wigs or hats!

YOU'LL NEED:
Medium-sized paper bag
Blunt-nosed scissors
Construction paper scraps, yarn bits,
   or buttons
Glue

✳ To make a paper bag wig, cut away the
front part of the bag, leaving some of the
paper in the front to make bangs. Cut
the paper bag into thin strips all the way
around. If you like, you can roll the strips
of paper around a pencil to make them
curl, or add flowers, ribbon, bows, or other
hair decoration to make the wig fancy.

✳ Here's a way to make a hat: Turn the bag
inside out, leaving a turned-up cuff on the
outside. Scrunch the bag into any shape.
Let your child decorate it with yarn, paint,
or markers. Your child could also dab it
with glue and add paper or fabric scraps,
buttons, and just about anything else to
decorate the hat.

YOUR CHILD IS WORKING ON:
Creativity
Imagination

Dancing to Music

Music can sound like romping elephants or blowing wind. Listen to instrumental classical or jazz music and watch your child's imagination soar—and arms and legs dance.

YOU'LL NEED:
Music
    Musical suggestions: Saint-Saens' "Carnival of the Animals," *Fantasia* Soundtrack, Tchaikovsky's "Nutcracker Suite"
Streamer, scarf, or towel

✼ Play music on a CD, tape, or radio and ask your child to listen and think about what kind of animal or feeling the music sounds like. Ask your child to move or dance the way he or she thinks the music sounds. Your child might want to pretend about these ideas with the streamer or scarf:

    an elephant with a long trunk
    the blowing wind
    a butterfly
    a tightrope walker

✼ Play music with a different tempo and feeling and invite your child to dance in a way that matches the new music.

YOUR CHILD IS WORKING ON:
Coordination
Listening skills
Pretending
Imagination

Puppet Play

Puppets come in many forms, shapes, and sizes. Because they're held an arm's length away, they can take on personalities of their own. At a comfortable distance, the puppets are really parts of a child's own personality that might not otherwise be expressed.

On the pages that follow, you'll find ideas for several kinds of homemade puppets. Here are some suggestions to help your child get comfortable with puppet play:

✳ Start by talking *about* the puppet—what it is, what it's made of, how it feels, what kind of puppet it might be.

✳ Slip the puppet on your hand or hold it and begin talking *to* the puppet, telling it about your child or something that has happened that day.

✳ As your child becomes more interested in the puppet's reaction, then you can begin talking *for* the puppet, answering the questions you ask, and turning the puppet to talk with your child as well.

✳ When your child seems comfortable, let your child have his or her puppet talk to yours.

✳ Here are a few suggestions to get puppet play started. The best stories are generally the ones that come from you and your child as you play together.

> Everyday experiences in a puppet family as they wake up, eat, or do other daily routines
>
> Taming a scary puppet
>
> A new child comes to your neighborhood
>
> The puppet is worried about starting school
>
> The puppet doesn't want to go to bed

YOUR CHILD IS WORKING ON:
Creativity
Imagination
Using play to work on feelings
Pretending

Spoon Puppets

YOU'LL NEED:

Wooden spoon or large serving spoon

Markers

Scrap craft materials
(yarn, felt, cotton balls, paper, etc.)

Glue

Handkerchief or square of material
(5 or 6 square inches)

Ribbon or yarn

✳ An easy spoon puppet can be made by just drawing faces on either side of the spoon, or gluing on bits of felt or scrap paper. Yarn or cotton balls glued to the top of the spoon can become hair.

✳ For a more elaborate puppet, cover the spoon handle with a handkerchief or square of material, fastening it in place on the neck of the spoon with ribbon or yarn.

Stick Puppets

YOU'LL NEED:

Small paper plates

Crayons or markers

Straws, popsicle sticks, or tongue depressors

Scrap craft materials (yarn, paper, fabric, buttons, etc.)

Glue

Magazine pictures or drawings (optional)

✳ Have your child draw faces on small paper plates and then decorate them with scrap materials. For example, buttons can be eyes and yarn can be hair. Your child might want to decorate several plates with different facial expressions to show different feelings.

✳ Attach the paper plates to straws, tongue depressors, or popsicle sticks to make puppets.

✳ Your child can make another kind of stick puppet by taping a drawing or magazine picture to a stick.

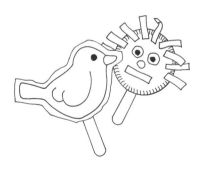

Paper Cup Puppets

YOU'LL NEED:

Paper cup
Scrap craft materials
   (buttons, yarn, paper, etc.)
Markers

✳ Put the paper cup on your child's finger.

✳ Make a hole in the paper cup big enough
   for your child to poke a finger through—
   the finger will be the puppet's nose.

✳ Use buttons, yarn, or paper to make the
   puppet's other features, or your child can
   draw on the cup with markers or crayons.

✳ To make simple clothes for the puppet,
   make three holes in a piece of cloth big
   enough for your child's thumb, pointer, and
   third finger to fit through. Put the cloth
   over your child's hand, and stick your
   child's pointer finger into the hole in the
   paper cup. Your child's thumb and third
   finger can act as the puppet's hands.

Sock Puppets

YOU'LL NEED:

Sock
Scrap craft materials (buttons, paper,
   fabric, yarn, etc.)
Glue

✳ Show your child how to slip a sock over
   his or her hand, with knuckles in the heel.

✳ Make a mouth by tucking the toe end
   between your fingers and thumb.

✳ Sew or glue on scrap materials to make
   eyes, nose, and hair. Be sure to let the glue
   dry before your child uses the puppet.

Puff Ball
Finger Puppets

YOU'LL NEED:

Cotton balls

Felt, handkerchief, or other fabric

Yarn or pipe cleaner

Popsicle stick or unsharpened pencil

Paper scraps, buttons

Glue

Markers

✳ Cover several cotton balls with a piece of felt, a handkerchief, or fabric.

✳ Gather the material below the puff ball with yarn or a pipe cleaner to make the neck. Tie the neck loosely so your child will be able to slip the puppet head over a finger, or attach it to a popsicle stick.

✳ Have your child draw simple features on the puppet's face with a marker, or cut the features from paper or felt and sew or glue them on the puppet.

✳ Some children like to make two or three finger puppets, so they can pretend to make them talk to one another.

Pretending with puppets is often a safe way for children to talk about things that concern them. They will sometimes allow puppets to say or do things they would never say or do themselves. Behind this safe facade, they can test out their feelings and our reactions. Whether it's puppets or other kinds of playthings, whatever you and your child create together takes on more significance because of its association with you and your relationship.

Box Puppets

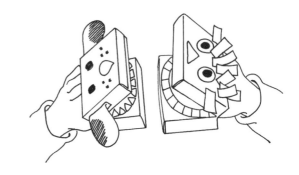

YOU'LL NEED:

Small empty box (pudding, gelatin, or
    single-serving cereal box)
Knife or scissors
Tape
Construction paper
Scrap craft materials (buttons, yarn,
    cotton balls, etc.)
Markers
Glue

✳ If you opened the box through a top flap,
tape it shut again. Then cut the box around
the middle on three sides.

✳ Fold the box along the fourth side to make
a hinge that looks like a mouth.

✳ Show your child that his or her fingers will
fit in the top part of the box, and place his
or her thumb in the bottom to make the
mouth open and shut.

✳ Have your child cover the box with pieces
of construction paper and glue on scrap
materials to make a face, hair, and mouth.

> **Younger children are often fascinated
> with puppets with mouths because they
> can use the puppets to pretend about
> talking, and also about other things
> like biting and gobbling people up.
> One task of growing up is learning to
> use our teeth to chew food, but not to
> bite other people. Most small children
> are likely to have angry times when
> they feel like biting, but little by little,
> they can tame those feelings, often
> by letting them out in puppet play.**

Helping

Working on responsibility

One day the "Neighborhood" mail contained a particularly delightful surprise—a package of messages from a preschool class. The teacher had asked the children to draw and talk about what makes them feel happy and what makes them feel sad. She told them she'd send the messages on to me.

Among them was this treasure from a young girl who said, "I'm happy when I get mom the toilet paper when she calls out from the bathroom!" No wonder she was happy—she was asked to do something she was able to do, and something that her mother obviously appreciated.

When children know their help is valuable, they feel valued, and naturally they're likely to do helpful things for us and for others in the future.

Taking on responsibility

When babies are young, they depend on us to take care of practically all of their needs. We're the "helpers." Then comes a moment, usually in toddlerhood, when children grab the spoon to feed themselves or insist on trying to dress themselves. "Me do it!" The food may be in more places than the mouth. The shirt may be on backwards, the pants sideways, the socks dangling off the toes, but how proud children are when they find out they can take care of some of their own needs, no matter how primitive their attempts may be!

With our encouragement, little by little children can take on more and more responsibility for themselves. They can begin by picking out their clothes or putting toys away. They can also do simple chores that help the whole family. What a good feeling it can be for them to know that it's not only adults who are the "helpers," but that children can be "helpers" too!

Feeling grownup

When children do grownup things, like setting a table, sorting laundry, or vacuuming the floor, they feel more grownup. In the long road toward independence, they need those small steps along the way to feel competent, capable, and more confident. What a good feeling it can be for children to know they're accomplishing something helpful and contributing in their own way to the family.

Working with you

We can't really expect young children to do too much on their own, especially when it comes to chores around the house. Because of safety reasons and because of preschoolers' own limited abilities, they need assistance from adults. As you work together, you will gain a "helper," and your child will gain that good feeling of working at your side. You might also learn more about your child in that time that you're spending together.

Do you know what else can happen when we adults use activities like the ones in this chapter to add a childhood sense of playful helpfulness to everyday household "chores?" We might just rediscover more of that child within us and see the playfulness carrying over to other so-called chores of our lives.

Laundry Matching

Any time that you're doing the laundry is a chance for sorting and matching games with your child.

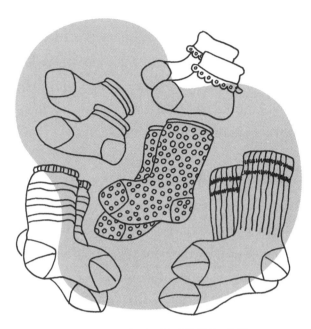

YOU'LL NEED:
Laundry to be sorted

✳ Show your child how you sort the laundry before putting it into the washer. Can your child sort into the piles of whites, darks, or bright colors? Things that are delicate or things that are sturdy?

✳ After the laundry is done, show your child that the clothes need to be sorted from each other again, but in different ways, when they're clean and it's time to put them away. For example, the white T-shirts or blue jeans need to be sorted according to size.

✳ Can your child pair up the socks?

✳ Ask your child to put each stack of clothing into the room where it belongs.

YOUR CHILD IS WORKING ON:
Responsibility
Classifying
Recognizing likeness and difference

As preschoolers are exposed to more things, people, and experiences, they try to make sense of the world by organizing things into categories. At this time in their lives, matching and sorting games can be especially appealing.

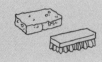

Clean-Up Magic

Here's a way to put some fun in clean-up time and to make it feel more manageable.

YOU'LL NEED:
Pieces of paper or index cards
Pencil or pen
Music from a tape or radio (optional)

✳ It's natural for young children to feel overwhelmed when they're asked to clean up their rooms. Sometimes a job feels more manageable when it is broken down into smaller specific tasks. Ask your child to help you come up with a list of things that need to be done to make the room clean. Here are some ideas:

> Pick up books
> Straighten the sheets and blanket
> Put dirty clothes in the laundry
> Put toys in their places

✳ Write each job on a separate piece of paper or on a separate index card.

✳ As if you're doing a magic trick, hold the papers (face down) fanned out like a deck of cards. You might even make a drum roll sound and ask your child to pick one card.

✳ Read the task aloud. For example, "Put the books on the bookshelf." Watch your child make the books "disappear" from the floor.

✳ When each task is done, ask your child to pick a new card. Pick a card for yourself, too.

✳ Another fun approach might be to turn on the radio, a tape, or CD and help your child put things away to the rhythm of the music.

YOUR CHILD IS WORKING ON:
Responsibility
Breaking down overwhelming tasks
  into smaller parts

Children might worry that you will expect them to do all the work of cleaning up. If you work *with* your child, doing one chore while your child does another, the time will go faster, and you'll have some fun together.

    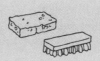

A Book of Coupon Gifts

Children can give help as well as receive it. Even young children have things they can do that are helpful in the family.

YOU'LL NEED:
Several sheets of paper
Blunt-nosed scissors
Markers or crayons
Stapler

✳ Start by cutting or tearing each piece of paper in half to make blank coupons.

✳ Ask your child to come up with ideas for ways that he or she can help the family. You or your child can write each idea on a coupon, or your child might want to draw a picture of each job. Here are some suggestions:

>Play quietly so a parent can have some peaceful time
>Give a hug
>Sort socks in the laundry
>Put out napkins for a meal

✳ Staple the coupons together, and let your child keep the coupon book. Then on special occasions, birthdays, holidays, or just any day, your child can give one of the coupons as a gift to someone in the family.

YOUR CHILD IS WORKING ON:
Responsibility
Literacy
Creativity

We give help, and we receive help, no matter how old or how young we are. As you work with your child to make coupons, you might want to make some of your own to give. In your own coupon book, you might include coupons for time with a parent, a treat at the ice cream store, or a backrub.

Washing Toys

Scrub-a-dub-dub! Turn a chore into irresistible water play.

YOU'LL NEED:
2 plastic dishpans
Water
Soap
Plastic tablecloth (optional)
Towels
Cloths or sponges
Old toothbrushes or scrub brushes
Washable toys

✳ Fill two dishpans with water. Add soap to one, and keep the other for rinsing. Set the dishpans on a plastic tablecloth or towel on the kitchen floor, bathtub, or sink. If the weather is warm, you could take the dishpans outdoors. Lay out a towel where the wet toys can be set to dry.

✳ Show your child how to wash his or her toys in the soapy water, and then how to rinse the toys in another dishpan.

✳ You may want to sing the children's folk song, "This is the way we wash our clothes . . ." Your child might want to make up other words to it. Here's an idea for the first verse:

> This is the way we wash our toys,
> Wash our toys, wash our toys.
> This is the way we wash our toys
> So early in the morning.

YOUR CHILD IS WORKING ON:
Responsibility
Independence

Water play is like a magnet for many children. Maybe it's attractive because it doesn't put pressure on a child to "make something." Water play can even help children work on toilet training because they are learning to control their body fluids.

What's Your Job?

Turn everyday chores into a game of chance, and find fun in sharing the work.

YOU'LL NEED:
Large piece of paper or cardboard
Game spinner (see instructions on page 18)
Name tags
Tape

✻ On the paper or cardboard, list jobs everyone in the family can do and put the list where everyone can see it. Even a preschooler can help with some household chores, like:

> Sponge the table
> Put out napkins or spoons for a meal
> Water plants
> Pick up toys
> Help wash the car
> Sweep the rug

✻ Beside each job, write a number that corresponds to the numbers on a spinner.

✻ Take turns spinning the spinner to assign a job for the week to everyone in the family. Tape the corresponding name tag next to the chore on the chart.

✻ Remember that when you praise your children for being helpful, you are helping them feel proud of taking on responsibility.

YOUR CHILD IS WORKING ON:
Responsibility
Literacy
Number recognition

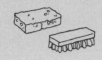

Milkshake Shake!

Milkshakes are usually made by machines, but they can also be made by hand. Let your child help and find a tasty reward at the end.

YOU'LL NEED:

1 quart plastic jar or container with a tight-fitting lid

Paper or plastic cups

Straws

Ingredients:

¾ scoop of ice cream (more if you want a thicker milkshake)

1 cup of milk

Will make about 2 cups of milkshake.

* Scoop ice cream into a jar or plastic container. Add milk.

* Make sure the lid is on tightly, then let your child shake the container until the lumps of ice cream are dissolved.

* You can then pour the milkshake into cups and enjoy a treat that you've made together.

YOUR CHILD IS WORKING ON:

Appreciating the value of work

Awareness of science (how solids can change into liquids)

Measuring

When you're preparing a meal or snack, think about what parts of the work your child may be able to do. Being invited to be an "assistant chef" can make children feel proud, as well as more willing to try some new food they've helped prepare.

Playing Restaurant

Let your child help turn an ordinary meal into something special. Here's a great idea for leftover night or when your child invites a friend over for a meal.

YOU'LL NEED:
Menus made on paper
Pad and pencil
Chef hat (see page 35)
Tray
Play money or pretend credit cards

✳ Decide what food to serve, then work with the children to write the menus. If you have a young child, you'll probably have to do the writing, or your child can draw pictures for the different foods.

✳ Talk with the children about jobs in the restaurant. Ask them to choose a position. Someone might have to double up on duties, just like in some real restaurants. The positions can be:

> Waiter/waitress (hand out menus, take food orders)
> Busboy/girl (set the table, clear the table after the meal)
> Chef (cook the food)
> Cashier (take money, make change)

✳ While you're giving the children a fun way to be involved with getting the meal ready and cleaning up, you're also giving them the opportunity to try different roles and see things from a different perspective.

YOUR CHILD IS WORKING ON:
Responsibility
Cooperation
Dramatic play
Literacy
Imagination

> **If you've written the words for the menu, your child is reading even if he or she knows only the first letter of the word. "Reading" pictures on a menu is also a beginning step towards reading words.**

Neighborhood Helpers

Helping isn't just something we do at home. There are lots of people who do important jobs that help a whole neighborhood or town.

YOU'LL NEED:
Magazines or newspapers
Blunt-nosed scissors
Paste
Blank paper
Stapler

* Have your child look through some magazines and/or newspapers and ask him or her to find pictures of community helpers, like:

> Office worker
> Mail carrier
> Truck driver
> Doctor, dentist, nurse
> Teacher
> Waitress, waiter, or chef

* Paste the pictures onto the blank paper and write the names of the jobs next to the pictures.

* Staple the pages together, and you've made a book.

YOUR CHILD IS WORKING ON:
Appreciating people who help
Learning about different jobs
Literacy
Dexterity

When children know that everyone's job is important, they gain an appreciation for people and value all kinds of work. They can also feel more secure knowing that many people help take care of them and their family.

Things that Go

Making playthings

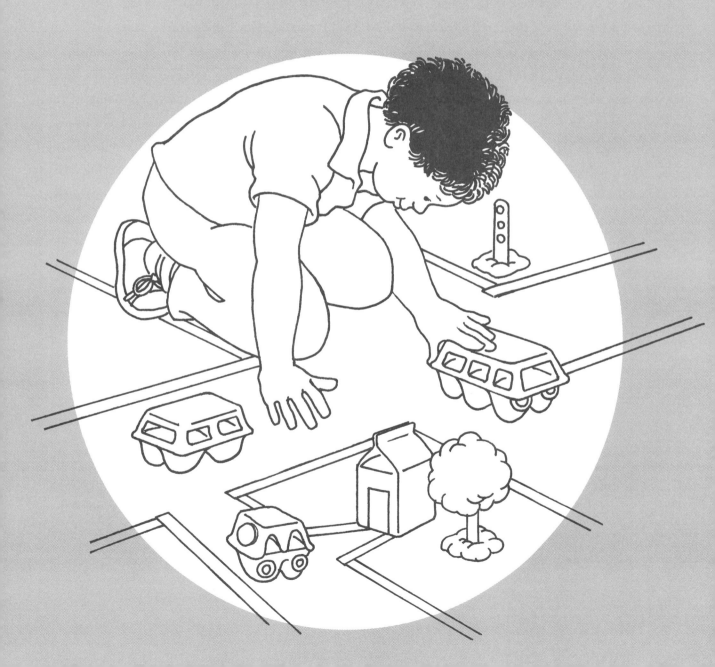

A friend of mine has a three-year-old son who is fascinated with trucks. "Trucks! That's all David talks about day and night!" his mother told me. "When we're looking at a book, he's interested only if there's a truck on the page, even if it's just a tiny toy on a shelf in the background. At bedtime, he won't go to sleep until he's recited a list of all the trucks he saw that day. It seems like trucks are all he thinks about."

Delighting in movement

Boys and girls can be fascinated by all sorts of things that move. An attraction to cars, trucks, buses, and trains usually begins at the same time children start crawling or walking. They're so intensely involved in learning how to get

around that they can be captivated by anything suggesting movement, or anything they can move smoothly along the floor or table top.

Many vehicles go fast, whether they're on wheels, in the air, or on water—and they move with such ease! What a delight they are to play with, especially for children who are just learning to walk and run—or who have recently done a lot of falling and getting back up and trying again!

Feeling powerful

Powerful vehicles like trains, trucks, and construction vehicles can become fascinating to children as they come to recognize that, instead of being at the center of the universe, they're not in charge of much at all. They don't have control over when to eat, how long they stay at the playground, or when they go to bed—someone else makes those decisions. Children can find real comfort in being in charge of playthings that are symbols of power—like trucks, cars, buses, trains, planes, bulldozers, and backhoes.

Developing self-control

With all their speed, vehicles have to be driven with caution—trains and trolleys need tracks, cars and buses need to stay on the road. When children play with toy vehicles, they can work on their own inner controls—their growing ability to stop and start and stay on track. Making a toy car stop can be a fun way to play about self-control. I've seen children "lock" their cars in toy garages (made from a cardboard box), maybe a symbolic move to keep their own negative urges locked up tight!

Dealing with feelings

When children are angry or frustrated or disappointed, you might find them crashing their trucks and cars into each other. While this looks like violent play and can make some adults uncomfortable, it can be a healthy way to express aggression on inanimate objects instead of people.

Coming and going

I know a girl who used a toy car to help whenever she felt lonely or sad. She would run the car up her arms, all the way up to the top of her head, saying, "Bye-bye. I'm goin' away." Then she'd roll it back down again, saying, "Going home now."

Playing with vehicles that take people away and bring them back is a way of giving expression to children's fears of being separated from people they love. Making toy cars, trucks, boats, and planes go away and come back again gives children a chance to work through some of their feelings about separation and return. What's more, in their play, they're in charge of who goes away, who comes back, and when! Cars, boats, and planes can indeed be "vehicles" for lots of healthy growth.

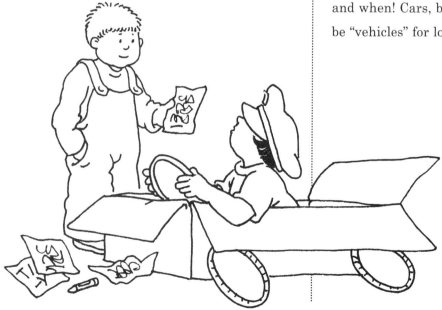

Egg Carton Cars

*Turn an empty egg carton into a car
to zoom around the room.*

YOU'LL NEED:
Blunt-nosed scissors
Styrofoam or cardboard egg carton
Garbage bag twist ties
Glue
Marker
Cardboard box (optional for garage)
Plastic wrap (optional)

✳ Start by cutting off the end of an egg
carton so that there are four egg spaces
for the wheels on the car. There will be
a hinge on one side so that the top can
swing open and shut.

✳ Next, cut the side and back panels to make
windows. Your child may want to use plastic
wrap for windows and windshields.

✳ Add a safety message by including seat-
belts in the car. Poke slits in the sides of
the passenger wells and thread twist ties
through the carton where the seats are.

✳ With another twist tie, make a door latch
to keep the top shut.

✳ Use a thick magic marker to draw shapes
that look like headlights on the front,
brake lights on the back, and spoked
wheels on the sides.

✳ A cardboard box can easily become a garage.

YOUR CHILD IS WORKING ON:
Following directions
Pretending
Dexterity
Imagination

Merrily We Roll Along

What things can roll? Wheels, marbles, balls? Children can, too!

YOU'LL NEED:
Blanket (optional)
Hillside outdoors (optional)

✻ Children can roll safely if they lie on the floor with their hands folded across their chests and roll over to the other end of a blanket or up to some piece of furniture across the room.

✻ If it's a warm, dry day, your child may want to use this technique for rolling down a hill.

YOUR CHILD IS WORKING ON:
Coordination
Observation of physical principles

While some children love the sensation and freedom of rolling down a little hill, other children may not like it. They may want to roll something else, like a toy car, down the hill.

Keeping on Track

Draw tracks and streets on an ordinary paper bag or old sheet, and you've got a place to play with toy vehicles—and a place to practice staying in-bounds. Keeping toy trolleys on the track or cars on the road can help children practice self-control.

YOU'LL NEED:
Several large grocery bags or an old bed sheet
Masking tape
Markers
Toy cars or homemade versions
Blocks or boxes for toy trolleys or buses

✳ To make a large mat for trolley or toy car play, tape several large grocery bags together or spread an old sheet on the floor. Draw a set of trolley tracks or roads on the mat with a marker, or put masking tape on the floor for tracks or roads. Older children may want to make their own tracks or roads.

✳ Have your child drive the toy cars or trolleys on the roads or tracks. Remind your child to keep the cars and trolleys within the boundaries of the roads and tracks just like people do when they drive real cars and trolleys.

YOUR CHILD IS WORKING ON:
Self-control
Coordination
Pretending

This can be a helpful activity when children are struggling with following rules at home, childcare, preschool, or school. This activity is also a fun way for children to use their fingers carefully to stay in the lines, an important skill for learning to write.

Building a Neighborhood

You and your child might enjoy building a whole neighborhood around the roads and tracks you create in the activity on the previous page. Here are some easy playthings to make to fill in the community.

* **Buildings:** Use milk cartons or cereal boxes covered with construction paper to create buildings. Add windows and doors by drawing or pasting squares of paper.

* **Tunnels and Bridges:** Cut cardboard oatmeal canisters in half lengthwise and set them on the ground to make tunnels for toy cars to go through. Blocks and cardboard boxes can also make bridges.

* **Traffic lights:** Paste three circles (red, yellow, and green) on each of several popsicle sticks. Put the sticks in clay bases to keep them steady (see page 92).

* **Stop signs:** Cut a piece of cardboard into several octagons and write the word STOP on them. Glue the cardboard octagons onto popsicle sticks and put them into play clay bases at the intersections.

* **Fire hydrants:** Paint corks red and glue them in the sidewalk area.

* **Mail box:** Stand a large-size kitchen match box on its end. Leave the drawer open a half inch or so at the top, and your child can drop "letters" in.

* **Shrubs:** Cotton balls painted green make good shrubs, particularly if you tug gently on the cotton to stretch it out and then spread it into clumps. Put shrubs into clay bases (see page 92).

YOUR CHILD IS WORKING ON:
Creativity
Dexterity
Imagination
Resourcefulness (finding new uses for things)

All Aboard!

Add some imagination to your kitchen chairs, and you've got all the ingredients you need for a pretend trip!

YOU'LL NEED:
Chairs
Construction paper "tickets"
Belts

✳ Let your child line up chairs in pairs or in rows. Friends or family members can pretend to buy "tickets" (imaginary tickets or tickets made from construction paper) to get a ride.

✳ Be sure to fasten your seat belts by putting a belt behind the chair and bringing it around to the front.

✳ If you're one of the passengers, you could pretend to look out the window and talk about what you see. You can stimulate your child's imagination by saying something like, "Look, there's a big truck next to us. What do you think is inside it?" or "That woman is all dressed up. Where do you think she's going?"

YOUR CHILD IS WORKING ON:
Playing about power and control
Coping with separation and return
Pretending
Imagination

Children often feel left behind when their favorite grownups go off in cars and planes. Before you go away, or after you come back, your child may want to use this pretend play to be in charge of who gets a ticket and who has to stay behind.

A Sailboat

Any kind of water play is a natural attraction for many children.

YOU'LL NEED:
Blunt-nosed scissors
Waxed milk cartons (pint or quart size)
Lightweight paper
Straw or stick
Modeling dough or play clay (see page 92)
Sink, bathtub, dishpan, or outdoor wading
    pool with water

✳ For the body of the boat, cut the milk carton from the base so that the carton has a bottom and is about 3" tall.

✳ Fasten the paper to a stick or straw to make a sail, then set it in place by sticking it into a piece of clay or modeling dough in the bottom of the milk carton.

✳ Now your boat is ready for its maiden voyage. Show your child how to blow on the sail, and watch how the boat moves through the water. You might want to talk with your child about real sailboats and what makes them move.

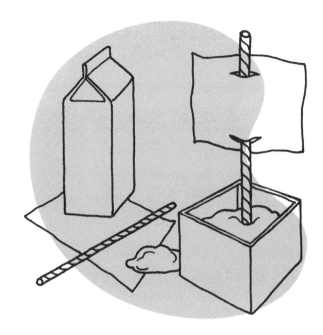

YOUR CHILD IS WORKING ON:
Awareness of science (learning about
    physical principles of wind)
Learning about cause and effect
Self-control

Children soon learn that the boat will tip over if it they blow on it too hard, so they have to use some self-control in blowing.

A Balloon Boat

Here's a "power" boat—powered by the air in a balloon!

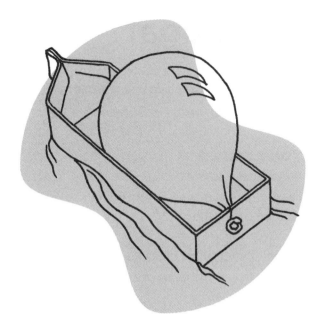

YOU'LL NEED:
Waxed milk carton (quart size)
Blunt-nosed scissors
Balloon

* Lay a waxed milk carton on its side with the opened spout facing upwards. Cut it in half, lengthwise, to make a sturdy hull for a boat from the half without the open spout.

* Poke a small hole in the back wall of the boat. The size of the hole will determine how fast the boat will go and how long the boat will glide across the water.

* Cut a thin slit down to the hole from the top.

* Blow up a balloon, and stretch it at the mouthpiece. Work it down the slit to the hole in the back wall, with the balloon inside of the milk carton.

* Keep the opening of the balloon pinched shut on the outside of the boat. When you're ready, let go.

* If you'd like, you and your child can try several variations of this activity, using different sized cartons, or altering the size of the hole in the back of the boat. Can your child figure out which variations go faster or longer? By experimenting, you may end up with a craft that moves really well.

YOUR CHILD IS WORKING ON:
Awareness of science (learning about the physical principles of air)
Learning about cause and effect
Dexterity

A Banana Boat

Most recipes require cooking or cutting or adult supervision. This is one of the few snacks children can make in the kitchen all by themselves.

YOU'LL NEED:
Slice of bread
Peanut butter
½ banana
2 thin pretzel sticks

✳ Spread the peanut butter on the slice of bread.

✳ Place the half of a banana on the bread.

✳ Fold the bread in half to make a "boat."

✳ Insert two thin pretzel sticks into the sides, like oars, to hold the bread together.

YOUR CHILD IS WORKING ON:
Dexterity
Pretending
Making healthy food choices

Row, Row, Row Your Boat

Here's a familiar song to use for exercise and muscle control, and it gives your child a way to have fun with words.

YOU'LL NEED:
Chair, blanket, or rug

✳ Show your child the arm motions for rowing. You could sit in a chair or on a blanket or rug on the floor and pretend to be rowing while you sing the song "Row, Row, Row Your Boat."

✳ For variation, sing and row slowly at first, then faster each time, then slower and slower.

✳ After you sing the original words for this song, you and your child might like to sing a royal version, sung to the same melody by King Friday XIII (ruler of the Neighborhood of Make-Believe on *Mister Rogers' Neighborhood*):

"Propel, Propel, Propel Your Craft"

Propel, propel, propel your craft
Gently down liquid solution.
Ecstatically, ecstatically,
Ecstatically, ecstatically,
Existence is but an illusion.

YOUR CHILD IS WORKING ON:
Coordination
Rhythm
Self-control
Language development

Once children have mastered a language, they often want to "play" with that language by using big words or even made-up words. You might want to use those new fancy words in everyday conversation with your child, asking him or her, "Would you like a glass of liquid solution?" or "I'm ecstatic over what you've just made."

Parachute Play

Flying or floating playthings move so effortlessly through the air. No wonder children are fascinated by them.

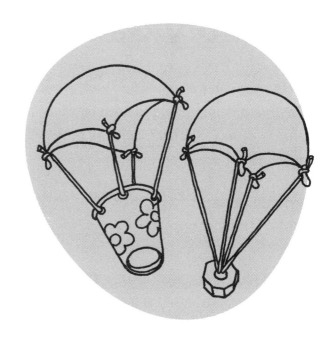

YOU'LL NEED:
Handkerchief or square piece of cloth
String (4" or 8" pieces for each parachute)
Small paper cups or metal nut/washer
Pencil

* To make a parachute, knot an 8-inch piece of string to each corner of a handkerchief or piece of cloth.

* Using a pencil, poke 4 holes around the rim of a paper cup and fasten the end of each string to the holes. For a different kind of parachute, tie the ends of the strings to a metal nut or washer, instead of using a cup.

* Your child can put toy people or small animals inside the cups—they'll add the necessary weight to make the parachutes float properly.

* Toss the parachute in the air, and watch it open and float to the ground.

YOUR CHILD IS WORKING ON:
Awareness of science (learning about movement of things in the air)
Following directions
Pretending

Memory Game

Bring out some of your child's playthings for this memory game to exercise your child's mind. Play and learning go hand in hand, in many ways!

YOU'LL NEED:
Toy cars or other toy vehicles
Table top or towel

✳ Put 3 to 5 (depending on your child's memory level) of your child's toy vehicles on a table or on a towel. Your child might have an easier time remembering the toys if you describe them as you put them on the table.

✳ Give your child some time to look carefully at the toys.

✳ Ask your child to turn his or her back, and take away one toy.

✳ When you're ready, ask your child to turn back around and tell you which toy is missing.

✳ If your child can't remember which toy is missing, ask him or her to look away again while you put that toy back in the line-up. Then ask him or her to identify which toy you put back.

✳ You and your child could take turns being the one who chooses the toy and the one who guesses.

YOUR CHILD IS WORKING ON:
Memory
Observation skills

Away We Go!

A cardboard box can be the start of lots of imaginative play—let your child sit in it, and watch his or her pretend play take flight.

YOU'LL NEED:
Cardboard box big enough for your child
    to sit in
Construction paper
Tape
Markers
Pie pan (optional for steering wheel)
Tin foil (optional)

✻ A box can become an airplane if you tape wings on it. You might want to help your child draw gauges on the inside front.

✻ To become a car, all the box needs are shiny headlights (from pie pans or tin foil and a steering wheel made from a pie pan or paper circle).

✻ With broom sticks or yard sticks for oars, the box turns into a boat!

✻ If you feel your child needs some help getting involved in this kind of play, try asking questions like:

> Where are you going?
> Who will be there?
> What will you see there?

YOUR CHILD IS WORKING ON:
Dramatic play
Creativity
Pretending

Feelings

Finding ways to express
all kinds of feelings

When I see children making angry paintings, dancing happy dances, composing sad songs, or taming scary puppets, I see childhood at its healthiest, for those are children's ways of expressing feelings.

Early on in my life, I found an outlet that worked well for me. When I was four years old, my parents told me I could choose what I wanted for my birthday from a toy catalog. When I saw the toy piano on one of the pages, that was it! Maybe I was drawn to music because I saw how much my grandfather enjoyed playing the violin, or maybe because I heard the pleasure that my parents and grandparents had in singing lullabies and listening to music.

Music soon became my way to express who I am. When I was angry as a child, my family wouldn't allow me to crash and stomp around through the house, but they did encourage me to play out my feelings on the piano. That's when I discovered the real power of music. I'd begin by banging random notes—anything, almost like punching at the keys. The longer I played, though, the calmer my music became, and the calmer I became, too. That piano probably got me out of a lot of trouble! To this day, I can still laugh and cry and express my anger through the tips of my fingers on piano keys.

Feelings are a part of being human, and when we encourage children to talk and play about their feelings, we are helping them find constructive ways of expressing their true selves—ways that won't hurt them or anyone else.

Talking about feelings

Whatever is mentionable can be more manageable, but young children often have trouble telling us what they're feeling. Many of them don't use words well yet. Sometimes feelings are a jumble inside and hard to sort out or to name. Through play, we can encourage children to put their feelings into words.

Being able to use words to describe what they're feeling gives children power over their feelings. Giving words to feelings can make them become a lot less overwhelming or upsetting or scary. Also, when children can talk about their feelings with a caring listener, they find out that their feelings are natural and normal, and that others have felt that way, too.

children have healthy outlets, they have ways to release some of the energy that is bound up inside.

What works as a release for one child may not work for another. It can take a while until a child finds some way of expression that's comfortable for him or her. That's why we've offered lots of different activities—music, painting, working with clay, physical activity—so that children can discover what feels right for them.

Developing inner controls

Self-control grows little by little and over a long time. Some of the activities in this section will allow your child to practice self-control to stop from hurting someone and to experience the good feeling of being in control of their actions.

Finding outlets for feelings

Have you noticed that you get tense and tight when you're upset, angry, or worried? There's a lot of physical energy tied up in feelings. When

Go-Stop-Go

Combine music with this "freeze" game to give your child a jazzy way to practice self-control.

YOU'LL NEED:
Music on the radio or tape

* Find some music on the radio or tape that's good for marching or other kind of spirited dancing.

* Tell your child to listen for the music—to march or dance when it's on and to stop moving when the music stops. (This works best if you can turn your back so your child can't see when you stop the music.)

* When your child manages to stop, you have a wonderful opportunity to say something like, "See, you can control yourself! Good job!"

* Remember, it's hard to calm down after doing a lively activity, so it's a good idea to play softer, slower music to help your child wind down gradually.

YOUR CHILD IS WORKING ON:
Self-control
Listening skills
Coordination

> Most children have trouble stopping in mid-air in the middle of a musical beat. It's even harder for them to control their hands from hitting when they're angry. Over time, your child will probably get better at this musical game, and that growing ability can extend to other times when your child needs self-control. When you notice the progress, let your child know you're proud of him or her. On our *Neighborhood* programs, we call that "inside growing."

Rice Cake Faces

*Round rice cakes make a great base
for a face that can show different
emotions and generate some healthy
talk about feelings.*

YOU'LL NEED:
Rice cakes
Spreading knife
Peanut butter or cream cheese
Raisins
Apple slices
Bananas

✳ Let your child spread a rice cake with
peanut butter or cream cheese. That's the
foundation for a face.

✳ What kind of feeling would your child
would like to make on the rice cake face?
Raisins could be used for eyes, noses, or
mouths. An apple slice can make a smiling
or frowning mouth. A banana chunk could
be a nose. A banana slice could be a surprised mouth or eyes.

✳ You may want to ask your child to talk
about what makes him or her feel angry,
sad, surprised, scared, or happy.

YOUR CHILD IS WORKING ON:
Naming feelings
Talking about feelings
Imagination
Dexterity
Making healthy food choices

A Doll as Big as Me!

Help your child make a life-sized doll—and work on an important life skill: self-control that begins with being aware of body boundaries.

YOU'LL NEED:
20 or more sheets of newspaper
Blunt-nosed scissors
Tape
Stapler
Marker or paint and brushes

* On the floor, tape two or three sheets of newspaper together to make an area that's large enough for your child to lie on. Make three more layers of the same size.

* Have your child lie down on the four layers of paper, then trace the outline of your child's body, from head to toe.

* Cut around the outline through all four layers. Staple or tape the four layers around the edges, leaving one side open.

* Gently stuff the outline with more sheets of crumpled newspaper. Leave two layers of paper on either side of the stuffing so the doll won't tear so easily. When the outline has been stuffed, staple or tape shut the open side.

* Your child might want to draw or paint features and clothes on the doll.

YOUR CHILD IS WORKING ON:
Self-control (through an awareness of body boundaries)
Pretending
Imagination

> **As you draw around your child's hands and feet, your child is having physical sensations that reinforce where his or her hands and legs end. In order for children to be able to control their hands and feet when they're angry (so they don't hurt anyone), they first need to have that clear sense of where their hands and feet end.**

Wheel of Feelings

Encourage helpful talk about feelings with this activity.

YOU'LL NEED:
Spinner (see instructions on page 18)
Marker
Magazine or newspaper pictures (optional)

＊ Make a spinner. Instead of using numbers, your child can draw a face showing a different feeling on each section, or your child could paste a picture of a person showing a different feeling on each segment. The spinner can include :

> Anger
> Sadness
> Surprise
> Happiness
> Fear

＊ Ask your child to spin the spinner, and pretend to show the emotion where the spinner stops with his or her face, body, hands, legs, and voice. You could expand this by asking your child to make up a story about someone who feels that way.

＊ If you keep the spinner handy, your child could use it to show how he or she is feeling any day.

YOUR CHILD IS WORKING ON:
Naming feelings
Talking about feelings

> It may help to remind your child that while we may know some things about how people feel by looking at their faces, the only way we can *really* know how they feel is if they tell us. No one can know exactly what we're thinking or feeling unless we tell them.

A Festival of Mad Feelings

This could be an activity for a day when your child has had a disappointment— like when a trip is canceled or when a friend can't come to play. Turn the disappointment into an occasion to give your child ways of expressing angry feelings.

YOU'LL NEED:

Play clay (see recipe on page 92)
Pillows
Drums or pots and pans
Crunchy foods like celery, apple chunks, or carrot sticks

✳ Before you start the Festival of Mad Feelings, give your child some rules, like:

> Play clay is to be kept on the table.
> Pound only the pillows, play clay, or drums—not people.
> When I give a signal to stop, you need to stop.

✳ It would be a good idea to begin with short time limits for pounding (15 or 30 seconds) to make sure your child can stop. Then increase to a minute or two of pounding.

✳ You could also set up areas for throwing pillows, for making a mad picture, or for making up a mad dance or song.

✳ For the grand finale, offer a snack of crunchy celery, apple, or carrot sticks for teeth chomping.

YOUR CHILD IS WORKING ON:
Finding healthy outlets for anger
Self-control

> **We can help children know it's okay to be angry but it's not okay to hurt. Through activities like these we can encourage them to find constructive ways to express those feelings.**

"Get Out the Mad" Cookies

These cookies taste better the more your child pounds on the dough.

YOU'LL NEED:
Large bowl
Cookie sheet
Oven preheated to 350°F
Ingredients:
   3 cups oatmeal
   1½ cups brown sugar
   1½ cups all-purpose flour
   1½ cups butter or margarine
   1½ teaspoons baking powder

✳ Place all the ingredients in a large bowl, and mix them well.

✳ Give your child a manageable chunk of dough. It's okay for your child to mash it, knead it, and pound it. The longer and harder your child mixes the dough, the better the cookies taste!

✳ When the mixing is done, show your child how to roll the dough into balls about the size of ping-pong balls, and place them on the cookie sheet.

✳ Bake the cookies 350°F for 10 to 12 minutes.

YOUR CHILD IS WORKING ON:
Finding healthy outlets for anger
Following directions
Literacy
Measuring
Patience

> **Following recipes involves reading and following directions. Your child can see firsthand how helpful it is to be able to read numbers and to measure carefully.**

Taming a Scary Puppet

By creating a scary puppet and then taming it, your child may learn to tame other scary things in his or her life.

YOU'LL NEED:
Paper bag
Construction paper
Blunt-nosed scissors
Yarn
Glue

* A paper bag is all you need to start making a puppet. Talk with your child about what would make the puppet look scary. Have your child paste eyes, a nose, ears, a mouth, and teeth on the puppet. Use yarn for hair or for a beard.

* While your child is making the puppet, you could talk about things that are scary for your child—like an animal's big teeth or loud sounds.

* When the puppet is finished, let your child talk with the puppet and find ways to "tame" it so it isn't so scary. You might suggest that the puppet is scary because it's sad or mad about something, helping your child to make up a story about the puppet's concerns.

YOUR CHILD IS WORKING ON:
Using play to work on fears
Talking about feelings
Creativity
Pretending

Some families find puppets to be helpful for children who have had nightmares or other scary experiences. But for some children, even a scary puppet is too frightening. If this is the case, you may be able to help your child make up stories about someone or an animal who was scared.

Note: For more on puppet play, see pages 38–42.

Not-So-Scary Shadows

Shadows can seem scary at night when children don't understand what they are. Turn them into playful fun in the daytime, and a way to offer some reassuring talk about other things that may be scary for your child.

YOU'LL NEED:
Bright light (such as a desk lamp or flashlight)

✳ Shine the light on the wall. Have your child stand between the light and the wall.

✳ Show your child how to use his or her hands, fingers, or body to make shadows. You may want to take turns making shadows and guessing what the shape is.

✳ You might use these or some of your own:

Make a deer by putting your thumb and forefinger together, with other fingers up for the antlers.

Make a rabbit by holding down your last two fingers with your thumb and putting your forefinger and middle finger up for the ears.

Make a dog or alligator with a big mouth by keeping the back of your palms together and moving your hands like a hinge.

YOUR CHILD IS WORKING ON:
Using play to work on fears
Talking about feelings
Pretending

Doctor Play

Playing about a visit to the doctor gives your child a way to rehearse some procedures that may happen there—to be the one in charge of doing the examination and giving the injection.

YOU'LL NEED:

Smock or old white shirt

A doctor's bag with some of the following:

    Tongue depressors

    Strips of cloth bandages

    Yardstick or tape measure
      (to measure height)

    Ballpoint pen without the ink
      cartridge (for pretend injections)

    Lightweight radio headphones with
      the wires hanging from them or
      an empty spool strung on a yarn
      (for a stethoscope)

    Plastic bubble wand (for checking eyes
      and ears)

YOUR CHILD IS WORKING ON:

Using play to work on fears

Role-playing

Pretending

* Doctor play is so inviting that it usually doesn't need much introduction. Many children like to examine their stuffed animals or dolls. Or you may want to pretend to be the patient.

> **Playing about experiences that might be upsetting or scary can help your child feel less helpless—and trust you more because of your honest and reassuring help beforehand.**

A Softee Friend

A soft cuddly stuffed "friend" can be comforting for your child to hold.

YOU'LL NEED:
Pillowcase (large or small)
Stuffing for the pillowcase—old rags, dryer
 lint, cotton batting, and/or foam rubber
Yarn
Buttons (optional)
Fabric scraps

❋ Stuff the pillowcase and tie it shut at
 the top with colorful yarn.

❋ Tie another piece of yarn around the
 middle for a waist or neck.

❋ Tie two pieces of yarn around the bottom
 corners to make feet.

❋ To make a face, you might use circles,
 triangles, or crescents of fabric for eyes,
 eyebrows, nose, and mouth. Does your child
 want the "softee friend" to look happy or
 neutral or sad or angry? Maybe your child
 wants to have two different expressions—
 one on each side of the pillowcase.

YOUR CHILD IS WORKING ON:
Using play to work on fears
Pretending

Sometimes a bit of comfort is all a
child needs in order to refuel before
feeling ready to move on. Just knowing you helped make this "softee" can
give it even more value at a lonely or
sad time.

A Sign of Growing

Here's a way to give your child the good feeling of pride for the small and big steps of growing inside and out.

YOU'LL NEED:
Paper (enough to make an approximately 11"x17" sign)
Pen or marker

* Tape the paper horizontally on the wall with the top of the paper at your child's height.

* Most growing charts show how much children grow outside. It's just as important for children to feel good about how much they're growing inside. On this one, you could note and date events, like:

> shared with a friend
> waited for a turn
> caught a ball
> used the potty
> cut with scissors
> said "I'm mad" instead of hitting
> rode a tricycle
> dressed without help
> wrote my name
> tied my own shoelaces

* If you make a new growing sign each month, you'll have a scrapbook of the many ways your child is growing.

YOUR CHILD IS WORKING ON:
Feelings of pride
Patience
Literacy

We all seem to make a fuss at the big moments of growing, like birthdays and first days at school, but what a good feeling it can be for your child to know you're proud of him or her at the little moments. Look for those moments to celebrate, like when your child is about to hit someone but stops. What an important time to say "I'm really proud of you." That's a great moment of self-control—a great moment to celebrate!

Creative Fun

Encouraging self-expression

One day in our office, we received a large envelope from Dallas, Texas. The letter, attached to eleven pieces of music paper, started out by saying: "Enclosed please find an opera, no less, written by a six-year-old viewer who was inspired by your programs." And there it was: a little boy's opera about an owl and a tiger and a king and an archaeologist who discover that what others thought was a monster was just a blinking flashlight caught in a tunnel. An opera by a six year old! Of course, his mother had written the words and the notes on the music paper for him and the characters are those he visits via our program every day—but the opera is his. He wanted to make one and someone encouraged him to try.

Most children don't write operas; nevertheless, every child is born with a unique endowment which gives him or her an opportunity to make something entirely different from everybody else in the world. You see it when you watch children at their own play. No two mud pies are the same. Block buildings have infinite variety. Paintings and dances take on their creators' touches, and later, hairstyles, jewelry, and language reflect individuality. When you see it all happening, you know something from inside is being shared with the rest of the world.

Each person has something no one else has or will ever have. Encouraging our children to discover their uniqueness and helping develop its creative expression can be one of the greatest gifts and one of the greatest delights of parenthood.

Creative materials

Hand children some raw materials, and they'll find their own ways to use them. You probably have lots of these materials around the house—maybe they're even throw-aways, like paper towel tubes, egg cartons, buttons, popsicle sticks, or shoe boxes. You might say, "Here's an empty box, what can you make from it?"

Having crayons, markers, construction paper, tape, or glue accessible can turn "What can I do?" times into "Look what I made!" times.

Responding to children's creativity

Because children need to know they're loved by the people they care about most, our interest and approval can play a big part in encouraging their developing creativity. But sometimes in our wanting to give encouragement, our enthusiasm can be counter-productive. Suppose Carla is angry at her brother. As she's painting her feelings of anger on the easel with large messy strokes of paint, an adult comes over and says, "That's very nice, Carla." Well, Carla might not mean it to be nice at all. She may mean it to be messy and ugly and "mad"—just the way she's feeling.

What's the best adult response? Quiet looking and listening—waiting for the moment when Carla might let you know what she wants you to know. There is so often much more than meets the eye! (And how much better that Carla could let her anger out on the easel rather than by hurting someone or ruining something.)

Process is more important than product

There can also be much less than meets the eye, as with young toddlers and preschoolers who are generally more fascinated by the process than by the product. When they paint, they marvel at how the paint drips down the papers. "Let me make whatever happens" they seem to be saying. It's much safer for adults to say, "Would you like to tell me about it?" than to ask, "What is it?" Children might say, "Nothing" or make up elaborate stories about their "drips." Either way, it's their "creation" to describe if they're so inspired!

We don't have to understand all of a child's creative efforts. What's important is that we communicate our respect for their attempts to express what's inside themselves. It's the creating that we need to encourage.

Stained Glass Windows

You'll probably find bits of crayon pieces in your child's crayon box. Instead of throwing them out, show your child a new use for them in these colorful window hangings.

Wax Paper

YOU'LL NEED:

Crayon sharpener or plastic knife
Old crayon pieces
Cardboard or sturdy portable surface
2 pieces of wax paper, approximately
   the same size
Iron

* With a crayon sharpener or plastic knife, shave off slivers of crayon onto a piece of wax paper placed on top of a larger piece of cardboard or other sturdy, portable surface.

* Let your child arrange the shavings on the wax paper, then cover them with another piece of wax paper.

* Carefully transfer the wax paper to an ironing board. Use a thin dishtowel between the wax paper and the iron.

* Press the sheets of wax paper together with a warm iron. The crayon shavings will melt and run together, making interesting designs. Don't let the iron get too hot—the wax will burn, ruining the colors and causing an unpleasant odor.

* After the wax dries, hang the design in the window and watch the light shine through it, just like through a stained glass window.

YOUR CHILD IS WORKING ON:

Creativity
Awareness of science (learning about
   effect of heat)
Dexterity

Colorful Containers

Here's a great way to reuse an empty can! Before you begin, make sure that the can you're using doesn't have a sharp edge that could cut little fingers.

YOU'LL NEED:
Empty can (i.e. from coffee, soup, yogurt, or frozen juice)
Cotton swab or small brush
Glue
Any or all of the following: yarn, construction paper, scraps of felt, tissue paper, magazine pictures

✳ Give your child a cotton swab or small brush to cover the sides of the can with glue.

✳ Let your child decorate the can however he or she likes. Your child might wrap yarn in coils all the way around the container, or add construction paper, fabric or felt scraps, bits of paper, or magazine pictures.

✳ When the glue has dried, your child might use the cup as a container for pencils, crayons, or toys, or give it as a gift to someone.

YOUR CHILD IS WORKING ON:
Creativity
Dexterity
Resourcefulness (finding new uses for old things)

Paper Mobiles

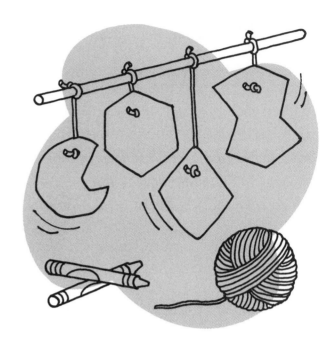

Paper mobiles are fun to make and fun to watch as they move in the air.

YOU'LL NEED:
Construction paper in different colors
Blunt-nosed scissors
Paper punch or sharp pencil
String
Coat hangers or wooden dowels
Crayons
Glue or paste

✴ Have your child cut or tear pieces of the colored paper into shapes or glue several shapes together, one on top of the other, for a 3D effect.

✴ Poke or punch a hole at the top of each shape.

✴ Tie a piece of string through the hole and fasten the other end to the coat hanger or dowel.

✴ Cut the string at various lengths to make a more interesting mobile.

YOUR CHILD IS WORKING ON:
Creativity
Awareness of science (learning about movement of things in the air)

Making a Book

Your child can be author and illustrator—and bookbinder!

YOU'LL NEED:
Cardboard (from the backs of tablets or
  empty cereal boxes)
Blunt-nosed scissors
Paper for pages (heavier paper works best)
Fabric
Glue
Paper punch
Yarn, shoelaces, heavy string, or
  notebook rings
Old magazines or catalogs
Crayons, markers, or colored pencils

✻ Make front and back covers by cutting two
  pieces of cardboard a little larger than the
  paper pages you'll be using. Your child can
  glue fabric to make fancy covers.

✻ Put 5 or 6 pages between the covers, punch
  holes along one side, and let your child lace
  the pages together with yarn.

✻ Let your child cut and paste magazine
  pictures on the pages. Maybe your child
  wants to draw pictures or make up a poem
  or song for you to write in the book.

✻ You may want to suggest a theme for
  the book or for certain pages, like animal
  pictures, my favorite things, alphabet
  pictures, or families.

YOUR CHILD IS WORKING ON:
Imagination
Decision-making
Dexterity
Literacy

Imagine how exciting it can be for
your child to "read" a book he or
she has made. Even naming things
in pictures can be an important step
for reading readiness.

Mix a Batch of Play Clay

Here are some easy, economical ways to make your own clay for all kinds of creative play.

PLAY CLAY #1

1 cup flour
½ cup salt
2 teaspoons cream of tartar
1 cup water
A few drops food coloring (optional)
1 tablespoon oil

* Mix the flour, salt, and cream of tartar in a small bowl.

* In a separate bowl, mix the liquids. Use the food coloring to mix your own colors.

* Combine the two mixtures and cook on medium to low heat, stirring until the combination is the consistency of mashed potatoes.

* When the mixture is cool, knead it a little. Store in a covered container.

PLAY CLAY #2

2 cups flour
1 cup salt
1 cup water
1 teaspoon salad oil (optional)

* Combine and mix all ingredients and store in an air-tight container.

* Keep in mind that toddlers might be tempted to eat the clay, so if there's a chance they may be around, it may be better to lower the salt content.

YOUR CHILD IS WORKING ON:
Following directions
Coordination
Creativity

Found Object Sculpture

Search your toolbox and catch-all drawers for raw materials to recycle for this activity.

YOU'LL NEED:
Popsicle sticks, tongue depressors, straws, or twist ties
Screws, nuts, and bolts
Modeling dough or clay
(see recipe on previous page)

✳ Have your child create a sculpture using the raw materials you've found around the house.

✳ If you plan to hang the sculpture on the wall, put a paper clip on the back in the soft clay before it dries.

YOUR CHILD IS WORKING ON:
Creativity
Resourcefulness
Dexterity

Children are fascinated with the feel of different textures and the look of different shapes. That's why "junk" drawers, with their bits and pieces of hardware items and other things, are full of treasures for this kind of creative play.

Yarn Pictures

It's like sewing a colorful design!

YOU'LL NEED:
Cardboard or Styrofoam tray
Yarn
Tape
Sharp pencil or paper punch

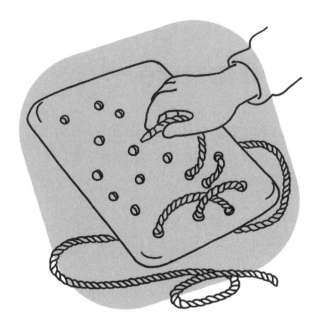

✻ Before you and your child begin, wrap the ends of the yarn with tape to make a hard tip that will thread easily.

✻ Using a paper punch or sharp pencil, make holes in the Styrofoam tray or cardboard.

✻ Show your child how to thread the yarn through the holes to make designs. He or she may want to use several colors of yarn.

✻ Encourage your child to try different ways of overlapping the yarn. Threading through the holes may be challenging at first, but you can reassure your child that learning to do careful work with your fingers takes time and practice. This might be an activity that your child does again on other days to see how much easier it becomes with practice.

✻ Some children might enjoy just drawing dots on paper and joining them in a creative way with a pencil, pen, or marker.

YOUR CHILD IS WORKING ON:
Creativity
Dexterity
Coordination
Persistence

This activity will give your child a creative way to practice the carefully-controlled finger movements that are needed for writing.

Flip-Flap-Fun

Surprises, like the ones under the flaps, can be fun for children when they are in charge of them.

YOU'LL NEED:
Two pieces of construction paper
Blunt-nosed scissors
Tape
Crayons or markers

✳ Give your child one sheet of paper and ask him or her to make a number of squares or rectangles. These boxes will become the "windows" for the other piece of paper.

✳ Using scissors, cut around three sides of each square and have your child help you fold the paper back. The folds can open like windows (vertically) or they can open like doors (horizontally).

✳ Help your child place the other piece of paper under the cut-out paper, connecting the two pieces with a piece of tape at the top for now.

✳ Have your child draw or paste a picture on the bottom sheet under each window.

✳ Tape the papers together on the remaining sides.

✳ Now your child can play "peek-a-boo" with the windows. Your child could also play a "concentration" game in which he or she tries to remember which picture is under which window.

YOUR CHILD IS WORKING ON:
Creativity
Dexterity
Memory

Musical Rhythms

Watch your child capture the rhythm of the music.

YOU'LL NEED:
Rhythmic music on the radio or CD
Paper
Crayons or markers
Play clay (optional)

❋ To help your child focus on the musical beat, start by moving or clapping to the rhythm of the music.

❋ Using the rhythmic beat of the music, have your child move the crayons or markers on paper. Your child might want to make swirls, long or short strokes, or dots according to the rhythm. Lots of interesting designs can emerge when creativity is sparked by the musical beat.

❋ Have your child make another picture to music with a different beat. See how different the design is when the music has changed.

❋ As a variation, your child can use the musical rhythm for play clay fun—tapping on the play clay with fingers, making ridges or other marks on it, or pounding on it.

YOUR CHILD IS WORKING ON:
Creativity
Listening skills

This is a different kind of creating because it's inspired by musical rhythms. Instead of focusing on the product, the focus is on the process.

Make Your Own Fruit Sundae

This sundae isn't made from ice cream; it's made from fruit. Offer a sundae glass or a mug, and let your child make his or her own creation.

YOU'LL NEED:

Sundae glass or mug

Apples, grapes, bananas, oranges, etc., cut in chunks and separated in bowls

Sprinkles

Granola, nuts, cereal, maraschino cherries, etc., for garnish (optional)

Whipped topping or yogurt

* Give your child a sundae glass or mug.

* Have your child make a sundae creation of his or her own, using the fruit, sprinkles, granola, nuts, maraschino cherries, or any other ingredients you may want to provide.

* Top it off with some whipped topping or yogurt, and *Voila!* A healthy treat.

YOUR CHILD IS WORKING ON:

Creativity

Making healthy food choices

Appreciating individual differences

Creative Collages

Colorful tissue paper can be an especially inviting material for creative play.

YOU'LL NEED:
Tissue paper in several colors
Tray or shoe box
Cotton swabs or small brushes
Liquid starch or diluted glue
Plain paper for the background

✳ Have your child tear the tissue paper into small bits, using a tray or shoebox to hold all the pieces.

✳ Using cotton swabs or small brushes, let your child paint the background paper with liquid starch or diluted glue (half glue, half water) and then arrange the tissue paper pieces on the sticky paper to create a design or picture.

✳ Your child might also want to make a similar collage with scraps of wrapping paper, wallpaper, greeting cards, or bits of magazine pictures or yarn.

YOUR CHILD IS WORKING ON:
Creativity
Dexterity

Paint-a-Cookie

Bring the "artist" into the kitchen for these fun-to-make, fun-to-eat cookies. If you prefer, buy pre-made cookie dough to make the project even easier!

YOU'LL NEED:
1 package of pre-made sugar cookie dough, or one batch of sugar cookie dough from a recipe
4 cups sifted confectioners' sugar
⅓ cup water
Food coloring
Pastry brush
Several small bowls
New clean paint brushes

✳ Bake the cookies and let them cool.

✳ Whisk together confectioners' sugar and ⅓ cup water, adding up to 2 tablespoons more water if necessary to make the icing smooth enough to spread.

✳ Divide remaining icing among the small bowls and tint each one with different food colorings depending on how many icing colors your child wants to use. Thin the icing slightly with more water if necessary.

✳ Your child can paint the cookies, using the pastry brush or paint brushes to decorate the cookies.

✳ Let the cookies dry completely before storing in airtight containers.

YOUR CHILD IS WORKING ON:
Creativity
Following directions
Dexterity

Nature

and Science

Appreciating the world

A mother told me about a walk she had taken with her three year old. "We were just going to the end of the street to the mailbox and back, but it took us a whole morning! Jamilla could have made it an all-day trip! First, she squatted down for a closer look at ants coming out of a crack in the sidewalk. Then she heard some birds above her, so we had to stop while she tried to find where the birds were in the tree. She kicked a stone into a puddle and watched the ripples, and then another stone, and another one! I never knew there was so much to see and do in that one little block between our house and the mailbox!"

Preschoolers are naturally curious creatures. They're engaged in a love affair with the world—as if they've suddenly opened the front door of their home and discovered there's a whole world in front of them. Even the tiniest things become fascinating to them. At this age, they're scientists, observing and experimenting. What a gift it is to us grownups, to see the world through our children's eyes! We might even find that things we took for granted are much more marvelous than we ever thought.

Curiosity and wondering

Children are hungry to know about the world. When we encourage curiosity, we're giving them one of the most important tools they'll need for school, and for life.

After they've mastered language, children often start asking a lot of "why" questions. They are ready to go beyond just naming things to using words to find out more about them. Children recognize that adults seem to know lots of things, so they ask us a lot of questions.

Of course, we don't always have the answers for our children's questions, and sometimes the answers need abstract thinking which is beyond the capacity of preschoolers. I've heard from parents who tell me that at times their children's "why?" questions become exhausting. It's helpful to tell children, "I can't answer that just now.

Let's talk about it later." Or, "I don't know the answer, or how to explain it to you, but that's a really good question." We're still valuing their questions and their appreciation for the world around them.

Attitudes are caught from adults

Just as our children can help to open our eyes to the marvels in the world around us, we can help foster their curiosity and appreciation; like the old Quaker saying: "Attitudes are caught, not taught!" Some of my deep appreciation for nature came from growing up in a small town, where there were many adults around who had a sense of wonder and respect for nature. I'll never forget my walks in the woods with my Grandfather McFeely. Birds, bugs, wildflowers, leaves, streams—they all remind me of the joys of being with him.

Haven't you found that one of the best ways children learn is from the example of the grownups they love? When children see that you wonder about and care for living things, when you marvel at a sunset or the moon on a particular night, that lets them know that you appreciate nature. And it's often quite contagious!

How Do Plants Drink?

Does your child know how plants get food?

YOU'LL NEED:
Celery stalks (including leaves)
Water
Jar or glass
Food coloring
Drinking straws (optional)

✳ Cut off about 1 inch from the bottom of a stalk of celery and show your child the little holes in the stalk. They are like skinny straws, packed closely together. Explain that the celery plant draws water up through the holes, the way we drink from a straw.

✳ Put some food coloring in a jar of water, and then put the celery stalk in the jar of colored water. After a few hours, the top leaves will begin to turn the same color as the water. Cut one of the celery stalks in half, and your child may be able to see the colored water in the veins.

✳ Now that your child has seen "celery straws" at work, you may want to put out drinking straws for water or juice at the next meal.

YOUR CHILD IS WORKING ON:
Awareness of science (learning how a plant takes in water)
Observation skills
Curiosity

Leaf Rubbings

Here's an activity that gives your child a different way to look at leaves.

YOU'LL NEED:
Several leaves from different trees or plants
Lightweight paper
Crayons

✳ Put a leaf under a piece of paper and show your child how to rub across it with the side of a crayon. Hold the leaf and paper still while rubbing the crayon across the paper. See how the outline appears, as if by magic. Rub some more, and you'll see the veins of the leaf.

✳ Try this rubbing technique with several different kinds of leaves. Ask your child to look closely at what is different about each of the leaf rubbings. Do some have jagged edges? Smooth edges? Do they have a stem going up the center? Do they have veins? What is similar about all the leaves?

✳ This activity can be a matching game, too. Can your child match the leaves with the rubbings?

YOUR CHILD IS WORKING ON:
Observation skills
Recognizing likeness and difference
Appreciating nature

As you help your child see similarities *and* differences in the leaves, you can also talk about how people are alike and different. Appreciating people is part of appreciating the world.

Homemade Toothpaste

Invite your child to play "scientist" and mix chemicals to make toothpaste.

YOU'LL NEED:
4 teaspoons baking soda
1 teaspoon salt
1 teaspoon flavoring (vanilla, almond, or peppermint extract)
Toothbrush
Air-tight container

✳ Mix the ingredients together to make homemade toothpaste.

✳ Dentists generally recommend that children brush their teeth for a minute or two. You might want to think of a familiar song to hum that takes that long, then sing it as your child brushes his or her teeth.

✳ Be sure to cover the container with a tight-fitting lid after each use.

YOUR CHILD IS WORKING ON:
Awareness of science
Dental health
Responsibility
Curiosity

This activity can give you an opportunity to talk with your child about what we do to care for our teeth, like:
• brushing in the morning and before bedtime
• brushing after meals (when we can)
• flossing to get out bits of food and to keep our gums healthy
• brushing or rinsing after eating sweet and sticky foods
You might find that your child pays more attention to dental care and brushing because you've worked together to make your own toothpaste.

Pumpkin Seeds

Children love to know about "hidden treasures" that are inside of things. Open a pumpkin and what do you find inside? Seeds that can turn into tasty toasted treats!

YOU'LL NEED:
Ripe pumpkin
Sharp knife
Large spoon
Paper towels
Vegetable oil
Cookie sheet
Oven
Salt (optional)

✳ Cut open the pumpkin and scoop out the seeds.

✳ Wash the seeds under running water, then spread them on paper towels to dry.

✳ Shake salt on the seeds, if you wish.

✳ Spray or spread oil on the cookie sheet. Then scatter the seeds on the cookie sheet.

✳ Bake in a 250°F oven for at least an hour for the seeds to dry out completely. Shake the seeds a few times. If you want, you can turn up the heat to brown the seeds for a few minutes, but be careful because they burn easily.

✳ Remove the seeds from the cookie sheet. Store in an airtight container so the seeds stay crisp.

YOUR CHILD IS WORKING ON:
Awareness of science (learning about seeds)
Curiosity
Following directions
Patience

Tele-Cups

Sounds can travel along a tight string. As the string vibrates, an earpiece on the other end will pick up the sound and make it louder, kind of like a telephone. Of course, the most important parts of a telephone call are the people who are talking!

YOU'LL NEED:

2 Styrofoam or paper cups, or containers
   from frozen juice or yogurt
Sharp pencil or nail
3' to 6' of string

* Poke a hole in the bottom of the cups with pencil or nail.

* Help your child thread the string through the holes. Knot the string inside the cups.

* Because the vibration of the string is what makes the phones work, make sure that the string is as tight as possible.

* Your child may want to experiment with Styrofoam *and* paper cups to see which one lets the sound travel better.

YOUR CHILD IS WORKING ON:
Awareness of science (learning about
   vibration)
Cooperation
Creativity

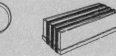

Shoebox Guitar

Show your child how to turn science into music.

YOU'LL NEED:
Shoebox (without the lid)
3 or 4 rubber bands of different sizes

✳ Help your child stretch the rubber bands across the width of the shoebox, and then show your child how to pluck or strum the rubber bands. The different sizes of rubber bands should make different sounds. You might even want to create an entire string section of a pretend orchestra using different sized boxes and rubber bands.

✳ You may want to add a cardboard tube to one end of the box to make it look like a guitar.

YOUR CHILD IS WORKING ON:
Creativity
Awareness of science (learning about vibration)
Listening skills
Recognizing likeness and difference

It's more than music you'll be making: you'll be encouraging an appreciation of sounds and science, helping your child develop listening skills, and most important of all, sharing some time together.

Let's Take a Walk

Children can find all kinds of treasures everywhere.

YOU'LL NEED:
A place to walk (sidewalk, yard, or trail)
Small bag or box (optional)
Magnifying glass (optional)

✳ Plan a walk with your child. You may not get very far, or move very quickly, but your child can have a chance to look for things like:

> Leaves, flowers, or plants
> Tiny bugs or stones
> Squirrels, dogs, or cats

✳ If your child likes to collect things, bring along a small bag to gather things that you find along the way. When you're back home, those things might become part of a collage or a mobile. Leaves can be used in rubbings. Stones can be painted and used as paperweights. Your child might want to keep the collection in a "treasure box" like a shoe box.

✳ Children who are interested in trees might enjoy a "tree walk." Help your child get to know the trees on your walk. Look carefully at their shapes and sizes. Touch the bark. Look at the shapes of different leaves.

✳ If your child is an explorer, take along a magnifying glass for close examinations.

YOUR CHILD IS WORKING ON:
Appreciating nature
Observation skills
Curiosity

> When adults go for a walk, we're usually on our way somewhere, and we walk at a steady pace. When children go for a walk, they stop and look at things around them. In fact, for them, looking is far more important than walking.

A Windowsill Garden

Most plants grow very slowly, and children don't have the patience to wait for a plant to grow. Here are some plants that grow rather quickly, so your child can see changes in a few days or a week.

YOU'LL NEED:
3 or 4 dried beans
Paper towels
Glass jar with lid
Water

✳ Soak the dried beans overnight in some water. This will make the beans grow faster.

✳ Line a jar with damp paper towels.

✳ Place 3 or 4 dried beans between the towels and the jar so you can see them through the sides of the glass.

✳ Keep the paper towels damp by adding a little bit of water to the bottom of the jar each day, as needed.

✳ Check the seeds from time to time for signs of growth.

✳ Within a week, the beans should sprout and start to grow. Eventually, leaves will begin to grow on the stem. Your child could make a chart to graph the height of the stem.

✳ If it's spring or summer, your child could plant the sprouts outdoors when the plants are about 2 inches tall. Your child can watch for changes that take place outdoors—more leaves, blossoms, and tiny beans. If the beans grow large enough, your child can open one and look at the new bean seeds inside.

YOUR CHILD IS WORKING ON:
Awareness of science (learning about growing)
Appreciating nature
Curiosity
Patience

Shiny Pennies

Watch a dirty penny turn into a shiny one.

YOU'LL NEED:
Several dull and dirty pennies
¼ cup white vinegar
1 teaspoon salt
Clear, shallow bowl (not metal)
Paper towels
Nickel

✳ Put the salt and vinegar in the bowl. Stir until the salt dissolves.

✳ Put the pennies in the liquid and watch them go from dirty to clean.

✳ Rinse the pennies well under running water. Set them on the paper towel to dry.

✳ Have your child then try this experiment with a nickel. You'll find that the nickel won't react in the same way as the penny because it lacks copper, the element that causes this chemical reaction to take place.

YOUR CHILD IS WORKING ON:
Awareness of science (chemical reactions)
Curiosity

> When we help children understand that the cause-and-effect relationships of science are predictable, they feel more secure and appreciate that the wonders of the world aren't just magic. One reason this experiment is great for young children is that there's a fairly simple explanation for why the copper gets shiny. Over time, the copper in a penny mixes with oxygen in the air and makes the copper dull in color. In the acidic vinegar solution, the copper separates from the oxygen, restoring its shine.

Me and My Shadow

Take advantage of a sunny day and go out searching for shadows.

✳ Go outside into the sunshine with your child. Ask your child to look for his or her shadow. What happens when your child moves? Can your child make the shadow dance?

✳ Look for shadows of different objects—cars, telephone poles, street signs, trees.

✳ You might want to share the classic poem, "My Shadow" by Robert Lewis Stevenson. Here's the first verse:

> I have a little shadow who goes in
>   and out with me
> And what can be the use of him is
>   more than I can see
> He is very, very like me from my
>   heels up to my head
> And I see him jump before me when
>   I jump into my bed.

✳ If you can, go outdoors again later on and see what your child's shadow looks like at a different time of the day. Where is the shadow? What does it look like?

YOUR CHILD IS WORKING ON:
Curiosity
Observation skills
Awareness of science (learning about the effect of sun light)
Literacy

Index

(for *The Mister Rogers Parenting Book*)

A

B

C

D

preparing for, 98–99

and regression, 97

L

Learning readiness

    basic concepts, 60–61

    in classroom, 61–62

    helpful hints, 63

    parents' expectations, 62

    through play, 60–61

    tools for, 61–62

Letting go, 86, 97

Limits, setting, 15, 31–35

Limits, testing, 15, 21, 31–32, 34

M

Mealtime

    conversations, 23

    as family time, 24

    helpful hints, 25

    problems, 22–24

    rules for, 25

Mister Rogers' Neighborhood, 16, 37–38

Moving

    discussing feelings, 100, 102–103

    helpful hints, 104–105

    parents' concerns, 104

    preparing for, 104–105

    and regression, 103–104

N

New babies

    arrival of, 82–83

    child's concerns, 48, 80–83

helpful hints, 82–83

parents' feelings, 81–82

preparing for, 82

and regression, 81

Nightmares, 45, 72

P

Parenting, 14–18

Pets

    caring for, 52

    choosing, 54

    as companions, 52–53

    death of, 54–55

    helpful hints, 54–55

    learning from, 52–54

    parents' attitudes toward, 53

    understanding, 52–54

Phases, 17

Picky eaters, 23–24

Play, learning through, 60–61

Playthings

    choosing, 26–30

    encouraging, 29

    helpful hints, 30

    sharing, 14, 57–58

Power play, 27–28

Power struggles, 15–16, 33

Pretending, 27–28, 30, 60–61

Professional help, 17, 116, 121

R

Reading, 60, 63

Real and pretend, 36, 45–46, 75, 111

Regression, 81, 97, 103–104, 111, 124

Index by Name of Activity

(for *Mister Rogers' Playtime*)

T

W

Y

Index by Type of Activity

(for *Mister Rogers' Playtime*)

This index is helpful for when you want to focus on a specific area of your child's development, or for when you're looking for an activity to fill a certain need. Here, the activities are listed by developmental benefits and by descriptive categories. For instance, if you are looking for something to do outside, you can look under "outside play;" if you are looking for an activity to encourage your child to read, check "literacy" for some suggestions.

A

E

F

M

N

Things to Save

Babyfood jars

Bottle caps

Boxes (cereal, pudding, cracker, etc.)

Calendars

Cardboard

Cardboard tubes (paper towel, toilet paper)

Catalogs

Cotton

Detergent bottles

Egg cartons

Empty spools of thread

Fabric scraps

Grocery bags

Jar lids

Magazines

Margarine containers

Newspaper

Paper bags

Paper clips

Popsicle sticks

Socks

Sponges

String

Styrofoam or cardboard meat and
    vegetable trays

Styrofoam packing material

Tin, plastic, and cardboard containers of
    all shapes

Used wrapping paper

Wood scraps

Yarn

Yogurt containers

About the Author

Fred McFeely Rogers is best-known as "Mister Rogers," creator and host, composer and puppeteer for the longest running program on PBS, *Mister Rogers' Neighborhood.*

His journey to the "Neighborhood" began in 1950, during his senior year at Rollins College, when he became intrigued by the educational potential of television. After graduating with a degree in music composition from Rollins, he joined NBC in New York as an assistant producer for *The Kate Smith Hour, The Voice of Firestone* and the *NBC Opera Theatre.* In 1952, he married Joanne Byrd, a pianist and fellow Rollins graduate.

Returning to his hometown area of western Pennsylvania in 1953, he helped found Pittsburgh's public television station, WQED, and co-produced an hour-long live daily children's program, *The Children's Corner,* for which he also worked behind-the-scenes as puppeteer and musician. To broaden his understanding of children, Fred Rogers began his lifelong study of children and families at the Graduate School of Child Development in the University of Pittsburgh School of Medicine. There he had the opportunity to work closely with young children under the supervision of Dr. Margaret B. McFarland, clinical psychologist. He also completed a Master of Divinity degree at the Pittsburgh Theological Seminary and was ordained as a Presbyterian minister in 1963 with the unique charge of serving children and families through the media.

Mister Rogers' Neighborhood made its national debut on public television in 1968. Since then, this pre-eminent series has been recognized internationally as a unique and pioneering effort to communicate with young children about things that matter in childhood. *TV Guide* says " . . . *Mister Rogers' Neighborhood* makes us, young and old alike, feel safe, cared for, and valued. . . . wherever Mister Rogers is, so is sanctuary." Fred Rogers has been the recipient of virtually every major award in television and education. He received honorary degrees from more than forty colleges and universities, and in 2002 was awarded the Presidential Medal of Freedom.

In 1971, Fred Rogers founded Family Communications, Inc., (FCI), a nonprofit company for the production of *Mister Rogers' Neighborhood* and other materials for children and families and those who serve them. Since Fred Rogers' death in 2003, FCI's ongoing work continues to be guided by his mission of communicating with young children and their families in clear, honest, nurturing, and supportive ways.

Play is the expression of our creativity, and creativity, I believe, is at the very root of our ability to learn, to cope, and to become whatever we may be.

—Fred Rogers